Transitioning Healthcare Support in Developing Countries From the US to China:

Emerging Research and Opportunities

Leo Eyombo
Howard University, USA

Renee Murray-Bachmann
Northwell Hospital, USA

A volume in the Advances in Human Services and Public Health (AHSPH) Book Series

IGI Global
PUBLISHER of TIMELY KNOWLEDGE

Published in the United States of America by
IGI Global
Medical Information Science Reference (an imprint of IGI Global)
701 E. Chocolate Avenue
Hershey PA, USA 17033
Tel: 717-533-8845
Fax: 717-533-8661
E-mail: cust@igi-global.com
Web site: http://www.igi-global.com

Library of Congress Cataloging-in-Publication Data

Names: Eyombo, Leo, 1972- author. | Murray-Bachmann, Renee, 1960- author.
Title: Transitioning healthcare support in developing countries from the US to China : emerging research and opportunities / by Leo Bachi Eyombo and Renee Murray-Bachmann.
Description: Hershey, PA : Medical Information Science Reference, [2021] | Includes bibliographical references and index. | Summary: "This book investigates what effects the USA and China have on supporting the healthcare needs in developing countries and how Africa has become a battleground of soft diplomacy in the international healthcare arena"-- Provided by publisher.
Identifiers: LCCN 2020027935 (print) | LCCN 2020027936 (ebook) | ISBN 9781799844501 (h/c) | ISBN 9781799844518 (eISBN)
Subjects: MESH: Delivery of Health Care | International Cooperation | Politics | Africa | United States | China
Classification: LCC RA441 (print) | LCC RA441 (ebook) | NLM W 84 HA1 | DDC 362.1--dc23
LC record available at https://lccn.loc.gov/2020027935
LC ebook record available at https://lccn.loc.gov/2020027936

This book is published in the IGI Global book series Advances in Human Services and Public Health (AHSPH) (ISSN: 2475-6571; eISSN: 2475-658X)

British Cataloguing in Publication Data
A Cataloguing in Publication record for this book is available from the British Library.

All work contributed to this book is new, previously-unpublished material.
The views expressed in this book are those of the authors, but not necessarily of the publisher.

For electronic access to this publication, please contact: eresources@igi-global.com.

Advances in Human Services and Public Health (AHSPH) Book Series

ISSN:2475-6571
EISSN:2475-658X

MISSION

The well-being of the general public should be a primary concern for any modern civilization. Ongoing research in the field of human services and public healthcare is necessary to evaluate, manage, and respond to the health and social needs of the global population.

The **Advances in Human Services and Public Health (AHSPH)** book series aims to publish high-quality reference publications focused on the latest methodologies, tools, issues, and strategies for managing the health and social welfare of the public. The AHSPH book series will be especially relevant for healthcare professionals, policy makers, government officials, and students seeking the latest research in this field.

COVERAGE

- Public Funding
- Access to Healthcare Services
- Assistance Programs
- Public Welfare
- Medicare and Medicaid
- Social Work
- Poverty
- Healthcare Reform
- Youth Development
- Social Welfare Policy

IGI Global is currently accepting manuscripts for publication within this series. To submit a proposal for a volume in this series, please contact our Acquisition Editors at Acquisitions@igi-global.com or visit: http://www.igi-global.com/publish/.

The Advances in Human Services and Public Health (AHSPH) Book Series (ISSN 2475-6571) is published by IGI Global, 701 E. Chocolate Avenue, Hershey, PA 17033-1240, USA, www.igi-global.com. This series is composed of titles available for purchase individually; each title is edited to be contextually exclusive from any other title within the series. For pricing and ordering information please visit http://www.igi-global.com/book-series/advances-human-services-public-health/102256. Postmaster: Send all address changes to above address.

Titles in this Series

For a list of additional titles in this series, please visit:
http://www.igi-global.com/book-series/advances-human-services-public-health/102256

Examining Gun Regulations, Warning Behaviors, and Policies to Prevent Mass Shootings
Selina E.M. Kerr (Independent Researcher, UK)
Information Science Reference • © 2021 • 196pp • H/C (ISBN: 9781799839163) • US $195.00

Practical and Political Approaches to Recontextualizing Social Work
Jacques Boulet (Borderlands Cooperative, Australia) and Linette Hawkins (RMIT University, Australia)
Information Science Reference • © 2021 • 325pp • H/C (ISBN: 9781799867845) • US $195.00

Digital Services in Crisis, Disaster, and Emergency Situations
Lídia Oliveira (University of Aveiro, Portugal) Federico Tajariol (University Bourgogne Franche-Comté, France) and Liliana Baptista Gonçalves (University of Aveiro, Portugal)
Information Science Reference • © 2021 • 411pp • H/C (ISBN: 9781799867050) • US $195.00

Epidemiological Research Applications for Public Health Measurement and Intervention
Simon George Taukeni (University of Namibia, Namibia)
Medical Information Science Reference • © 2021 • 214pp • H/C (ISBN: 9781799844143) • US $295.00

Global Issues and Innovative Solutions in Healthcare, Culture, and the Environment
Mika Merviö (Kibi International University, Okayama, Japan)
Information Science Reference • © 2020 • 366pp • H/C (ISBN: 9781799835769) • US $195.00

For an entire list of titles in this series, please visit:
http://www.igi-global.com/book-series/advances-human-services-public-health/102256

IGI Global
PUBLISHER of TIMELY KNOWLEDGE

701 East Chocolate Avenue, Hershey, PA 17033, USA
Tel: 717-533-8845 x100 • Fax: 717-533-8661
E-Mail: cust@igi-global.com • www.igi-global.com

Table of Contents

Preface

This book explores the history of healthcare in Africa from the 1960s to the COVID19 (Coronavirus) Pandemic in 2020. The journey examines the relationship between the People's Republic of China (PRC) and the United States of American (USA) in providing healthcare services to Africa. Healthcare has been used as a source to pawn for soft diplomacy. The perception of these healthcare services in Africa has really affect the relationship dynamics between these superpowers. There have been some changes during the last 60 years. The PRC has evolved to be a superpower and a major player in the international healthcare development arena. The USA has struggle to maintain its image as a major builder of soft diplomacy. These struggles are documented in this book and shows the areas of success and failure. Contrary, to the (PRC) developing a more aggressive action to maintain soft power diplomacy while changing their image among Africans.

Africa has also changed in the last sixty (60) years. The needs of the African continent has to be individualized, so as to meet the healthcare needs of individual countries. As the PRC has become more influential so has some situations of social conflict with the average African. These conflict have been a major hurdle in the PRC versus African relationship. The USA on the other hand has reduced international development funds and has been in a healthcare crisis of its own. Some of the hurdles documented in this book is racism in PRC and Chinese residing in Africa. While the USA government has been struggling with just managing the Coronavirus Pandemic that PRC has also been struggle maintaining their new status in Africa. The racism issue in PRC has been linked to the perception of Africans also rethinking their position in this relationship. Africans will be in a new place during and after the Coronavirus pandemic because of some PRC case of racism on the social media. Africa has really become the last battle ground for soft power with healthcare being the measuring tool.

Chapter 1

The history of international development AID in developing Africa. Most of these developmental project started in the 1960's and has been used as a tool for diplomacy. Healthcare for example has been a major tool for diplomacy by the United States of American (USA) and China (PRC). During this era, the USA was the leader of the soft power diplomacy and PRC was still a poor country trying to survive by making new friends in Africa. China's engagement in Africa health projects has differed from aid provided by traditional western donors. The PRC builds on its own prior experiences of building its own health system as a developing country, and in the manner in which it places special emphasis on the issue of the national sovereignty of recipient countries.

Chapter 2

The important of healthcare as a tool of diplomacy is documented and acknowledged. The West and China have common interests in Africa regarding economic development and environmental protection. China, Africa and Western countries must discuss effective methods for increasing cooperation on the continent together. But their interest can sometimes be contradictory in different aspects of the continent. Healthcare is the crossroads of their geo-political implications in Africa. As the PRC evolves from a poor country to a super power, Africa has become the testing ground for soft power diplomacy via economic development and health care.

Chapter 3

African public healthcare systems suffer from significant "brain drain" of its health care professionals and knowledge. As health workers migrate to wealthier countries such as Australia, Canada, USA, and the United Kingdom. While Africa is struggling to meet its health care needs; PRC is playing an increasingly important role in the African public health sector. However, only a handful of countries have received priority in receiving Chinese development assistance for healthcare. The USA has really struggle with the development of new strategies for international development. As the USA been reducing health care option in the development nations in Africa, PRC has increase money and expertise for Africa.

Chapter 4

International development of healthcare aid between the USA and China during the cold war. The best propaganda is no propaganda but a superpower should provide resources allocated, to developing countries during this information age to enable economic growth. While the United States and the Soviet Union were in competition during the cold war. Africa was been accommodated and charmed by the Chinese. The ability to rally support for China to be a member of the United Nations gave African countries some diplomatic muscle to build more complex relationship with PRC. The soft power dynamic between Africa and China grew while the major superpowers were fighting about arms expansion.

Chapter 5

The motivation of the Chinese on soft power economic development goes beyond healthcare diplomacy. Chinese firms and construction projects are all over the Africa continent. Across the Continent, American schools and hospitals has been in the decline while china hospital have sprung everywhere. The USA on the other hand has almost reduce its economic development hold on the continent while China has increased its involvement in global health governance. As the largest developing country and the second largest economy in the world, China's engagement in global health governance should be given considerable attention. China has been providing medical assistance in various ways to African now for almost six decades.

Chapter 6

As Chinese and African countries grow in trade and economic development so has the soft power dynamics. Healthcare has been an area where the Chinese has dominated the area for the last decade. The USA has been in a decline and has been absent in providing the leadership in health care soft power dynamics. The partisan politics in the USA has consumed the United States Agency for International development. Bringing us to era of Chinese experimentation with a free market (Capitalism) and toying with international development superpower status. Yet, there are still areas of improvement for health care in Africa between United States America (USA); China (PRC). Africans have become use to engaging with Chinese in the hope of meeting their developmental healthcare goals. But the acceptance of the Chinese health care and medicine in Africa is a game changer in the healthcare diplomacy arena.

Chapter 7

An estimated 1 million Chinese live and work in Africa. Many now face added scrutiny or outright discrimination, after social media picture of African being discriminated in PRC. These Chinese live in every country in the continents. As business has grown between Chinese and Africa so has the interaction between the two groups. Some of these interactions as mentioned earlier, have not been friendly. The geopolitical implication of international development health care in Africa is being shadowed by cultural differences. The state of international health care development in Africa and the scramble by USAID and the Chinese debate has been overshadowed by social media discrimination images. Non-traditional media has led the debate on the soft power control of Africa. as the novel coronavirus rages through the world and spreads rapidly in the U.S., Africa is the least-affected continent at the moment, with less than 300 reported cases in roughly half of its 54 countries so far. As the corona virus cases increased in Africa, this has becomes the new battleground for a new scramble for Africa.

Chapter 8

There has been a lot of changes during this COVID-19 pandemic that will affect the relationship between (PRC) and the African continent. Some of these changes has been in the interpersonal relationship between ordinary Chinese and individuals of African descent. These changes has really affect the diplomatic relationship and its effects on healthcare developmental projects. These projects have been affected by images on social media on, how the Chinese mistreat Africans in China. Social media has been an important tool to affect the dynamic in these relationships than non-traditional media. These social media outlet have been instrumental in the availability of mistreated Africans in the PRC, available 24 hours on people personal phone. The United States of American, The People's Republic of China and the African continent will be on a new era in diplomatic relationship after the Corona (COVID-19) Pandemic. Whoever will get the best game plan will win the heart and minds of Africans.

Chapter 1
Healthcare Diplomacy

ABSTRACT

This chapter presents a historical summary of international development aid in developing Africa as a form of diplomacy. Most of these developmental projects started in the 1960s after independence and have been used as a tool for diplomacy. Healthcare for example has been a major tool for diplomacy by the United States of American (USA) and now China (PRC). During this era, the USA was the leader of soft power diplomacy and PRC was still a poor country trying to survive by making new friends in Africa. China's engagement in African health projects has differed from aid provided by traditional Western donors. The PRC builds on its own prior experiences of building its health system as a developing country and in the manner in which it places special emphasis on the issue of the national sovereignty of recipient countries.

INTRODUCTION

Health diplomacy is not necessarily a new concept, but its use and application have shifted in recent years. Historically, health diplomacy focused on international collaboration to protect human and commercial interests against the spread of infectious diseases. It was less of a tool of encouraging closer relations among nations and more of a way to prevent commercial interruptions. The mere threat of bubonic plague or cholera was enough to close ports or impose quarantine measures, both of which impeded the exchange of goods and people (Novotny and Kickbush: 2008, Youde 2010).

DOI: 10.4018/978-1-7998-4450-1.ch001

China's engagement in Africa health aid has differed from aid provided by traditional western donors, particularly in the way China builds on its own prior experiences in building its health system as a developing country, and in the manner in which it places special emphasis on the issue of the national sovereignty of recipient countries (Lin et al. 2016). China's current approach to supplying personnel and infrastructure in a piecemeal way cannot substantially contribute to improving the health of Africans, says Ray Yip, formal director of the China program at the Bill and Miranda Gates Foundation. "Those all represent a substitution approach. [The Chinese] go to the hospital, they run the service of the year, and during that time people in the catchment area benefit. But when they leave, there is not much left behind. So it's not a bad thing but in terms of impact, it's relatively small. Even if they scaled up ten times, it's still going to have a limited impact" (Alcorn 2015).

Chinese medical support in Africa dates back half a century – in 1963, China sent 100 healthcare workers to assist Algeria after it gained independence from France. However, the level of involvement has been increasing in the past decade (Wang, 2018, Brautigan 2011).

Wang (2018) stated, in 2006, at the third Forum on China-Africa Cooperation (FOCAC), held in Beijing, Chinese and African officials introduced measures to broaden bilateral cooperation, including medical care and public health. The Chinese spent an estimated $35 million on health-related projects in Africa in 2006. By 2014, they were disbursing an estimated $150 million annually. Chinese parties build health facilities, donate supplies, grant funds, and provide staff.

Some 1,500 – 2,000 languages are spoken across Africa. Shen had limited English-language training and had particular differences in speaking with elderly patients, many of whom don't speak English. To interpret, he replied on younger generations and his mobile phone (Wang, 2018). Cynics have raised concerns, viewing Chinese aid as politically or financially motivated. Unlike US aid, which stresses domestic governance and transparency, China explicitly takes a noninterference approach. At the 2015 China- Africa Summit, Chinese President Xi Jinping said "Africa belongs to the African people and African Affairs should be handled by the African people.", (Wang, 2018).

Given China's involvement in Africa, there is an even greater need for the US to engage and cooperate with China for its national interests and global agenda, such as security and governance. Not engaging China in Africa could undercut and even nullify US objectives given China's approach. Cooperation on security issues, like south Sudan, most likely will not excite China in that China believes the US might ask Beijing to carry a disproportionate share of economic and political responsibility. Furthermore, China worries that a US – China/G-2 approach to Africa security issues might alienate China's traditional friendship with African countries since China prefers bilateral or multilateral approaches (Yun Sun 2013).

(Sun 2013); Stated there are key issues on which the US could and should focus. The US needs to raise its concerns and request that China adjust its investment and assistance policies towards Africa through the Africa consultation under the US-China Strategic Economic Dialogue. The US needs to better coordinate with China on providing aid technology and technical support in the fields of health care, and medical and agricultural assistance. Furthermore, inside Africa, the US needs to mobilize its political, diplomatic, and soft power influences to mitigate the negative impact of the mercantilist approach of China. Last but not least, a conscious educational effort should be made to help Africa achieve the long-term vision about the consequences of China's myopic development model.

According to Brautigam (2011) and Anshan (2011), while China began to provide foreign aid in the 1950s, its medical assistance to Africa was not launched until April 1963, when the first Chinese medical team (CMT) arrived in the newly independent Algeria. The decision to dispatch a foreign-aid medical team to Africa was largely driven by foreign policy considerations, which included the need to compete with Taiwan for diplomatic recognition. As a Chinese scholar observed, the evolution of the CMT program in Africa largely paralleled China's changing diplomatic ties with African countries. Total estimates range from around 580 000 to over 800 000 Chinese on the African Continent. By far the largest number of Chinese can be found in South Africa, followed by Nigeria. Sudan, Angola, Algeria, and Mauritius are only the other countries with well over 10 000 Chinese. There are approximately 400 000 Chinese in France; 600 000 Chinese in Japan (Park 2009).

In recent years, Africa has regained a level of prominence in China's overall foreign policy strategy. As part of China's renewed interest in building strong relationships with African states, the government has reinvigorated its commitment to health diplomacy programs. It has become part of the Chinese government's diplomatic arsenal to bolster its standing among developing countries, insulate itself against pressure from the Western States, and counter calls for greater respect for human rights and liberal diplomacy. Health diplomacy offers China a more subtle means of influencing states and gaining international stature (Youde, 2010). New orientation for China's health assistance to Africa. For five decades, China has deployed doctors and built hospitals in Africa. The country's leaders signaled a shift in strategy that might have a more lasting impact (Ted Alcorn reports, 2015).

One of the major challenges in understanding the scope and impact of China's health assistance to Africa is the lack of information regarding the amount of such aid (or its overall foreign aid), the criteria for making aid decisions, and the mechanism for determining the impact of aid (Lin, et al. 2016). Contrary, to the Chinese secret accounting in health international aid the Ebola crisis was an exception. These Ebola support figures were made public by the Chinese to show a mastery of health care diplomacy in Africa.

The Chinese government worked with the international community, humanitarian agencies, and frontline non-government organizations including African countries to contain and control Ebola epidemics in West Africa. Compared to other developed countries, China provided a robust technical and non-technical assistance to 13 countries in and around the affected West African sub-region valued at about $120 million (USD) and pledged an extra $5 million (USD) to the UN Response Multi-partner Trust Fund to support recovery and rehabilitation processes of the affected countries (Tambo, et al. 2016)

Modern Chinese diplomatic involvement in Africa goes back to the 1950s. During these initial interactions, China sought to frame its relationships with African governments and anti-colonial movements as a counterweight to the perceived hegemonies of both the United States and the Soviet Union. Unlike the Soviet Union, the Chinese government presented itself to African constituencies as a patron who rejected the imperial mandates of Western powers and understood the Unique struggles of "peasant movements". Sino-African relations in the 1950s and 1960s focused on the Chinese promoting Maoism as the most appropriate model for development and anti-colonialism. It is also provided financial, logistical, and training support for revolutionary movements on the continent (Larkins 1970, Youde 2010).

According to Larkin, Sino-African relations in the 1970s had five key characteristics. First, the number of African Countries with diplomatic ties gradually increased. In 1967, China had 13 diplomatic missions in Africa and by 1972 this number had increased to 30.

What all the countries had in common was their shared history and their perception of the white dominance by the West. Statements such as "we all belong to the Third World, we are developing countries" were commonly heard at this time. During the conference, China and the African States adopted the five principles of 'Peaceful Coexistence' that had earlier been formulated by India and China. These covered (1) mutual respect for sovereignty and territorial integrity; (2) mutual non-aggression; (3) non-interference in each other's internal affairs; (4) equality and mutual benefit; and (5) peaceful coexistence (Ibid, Van de Looy, 2006).

Following the conference, China supported African countries with economic, technical, and military support in an attempt to restrain the dominant western powers and create a new political and international order. The African States were at the same time seeking allies to help them win their fight for independence and financial support to fund these struggles. From 1966 to 1969, Chinese attention towards Africa diverted due to domestic changes and the great proletarian Cultural Revolution. After internal disputes had been settled, China began to establish new relationships on the African continent (Ibid, Van de Looy, 2006).

The impact of China's investment in Africa can lead to the shift of all resources that Africa maintained for centuries to be extracted and taken away by investors while the indigenous remains poor. In some of the areas where Chinese companies are investing especially in drilling projects and minerals, individuals are suffering poverty and fighting to improve social services like water, hospital, schools, and roads while the land is rich. The only problem is that these people have no enough education and capital to extract their resources. Contracts of China-Africa investment must be clear to both sides. The step will eliminate the concept among people who think that China is using a new methodology to scramble African resources. Africans must know their benefits of dual investments; otherwise, chaos will erupt within investment areas where people think that China is trying to invade Africa in a modern way like European countries in the 19th century after the Berlin Conference of 1884/85 (Ishengoma and Bo, 2014).

Researchers Lin, et al. (2016) China began its health assistance effort to support African countries, there is a paucity of information regarding its scale, scope, and impact. Irrespective of the nature of the assistance, there is the need for a systematic and rigorous evaluation of the various approaches and investments. Such assessments could be critical in informing future investments and consequently serving to advance the health of the target populations. In its more contemporary usage, health diplomacy is "political activity that meets the dual goals of improving health while maintaining and strengthening international relations", (Novotny and Kickbusch, 2008, Youde, 2010).

Table 1. African recipient countries and their starting year of receiving China's medical assistance

Country	Start	Country	Start
Algeria	1963	Gabon	1977
Zanzibar	1964	Gambia	1977
Somalia	1965	Benin	1978
Congo (Brazzaville)	1967	Zambia	1978
Mali	1968	Central African Republic	1978
Tanganyika (Tanzania)	1968	Chad	1978
Mauritania	1968	Botswana	1981
Guinea	1968	Djibouti	1981
Sudan	1971	Rwanda	1982
Equatorial Guinea	1971	Uganda	1983
Sierra Leone	1973	Libya	1983
Tunisia	1973	Cape Verde	1984
Democratic Republic of Congo	1973	Liberia	1984
Ethiopia	1974	Zimbabwe	1985
Togo	1974	Burundi	1986
Cameroon	1975	Seychelles	1987
Senegal	1975	Comoros	1994
Madagascar	1975	Namibia	1996
Morocco	1975	Lesotho	1997
Niger	1976	Eritrea	1997
Mozambique	1976	Malawi	2008
Sao Tome and Principe	1976	Angola	2009
Guinea-Bissau	1976	Ghana	2009

Source: Adapted from Li (2009).

Challenges Health Care in Africa

Trust is an essential component of the patient-physician relationship. Patient-physician trust affects a patient's willingness to see a physician, disclose information, and accept therapy, thus enabling the cooperation between the patient and the physician that is needed for effective care. Patients who trust their physicians are more likely to seek health care (PLOS, 2015).

Figure 1. A social-ecological framework for African migrant patients' trust of Chinese physicians (PLOS, 2015)

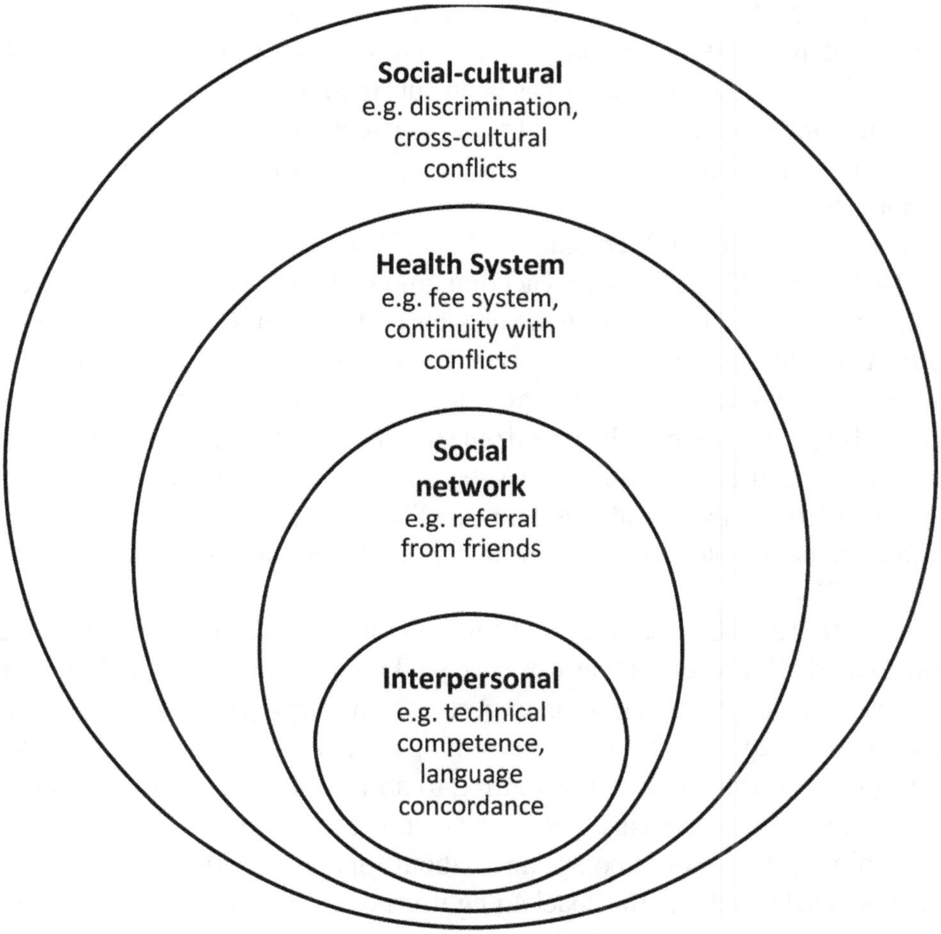

Since 1963, under the protocol on the dispatch of medical teams signed between the government of China and the recipient countries, about 23,000 Chinese medical workers have been sent to 66 countries to provide services to an estimated 270 million people. At the end of 2013, 1171 Chinese medical workers were working in 113 medical centers in 49 countries. 42 of these countries are in Africa, and the remaining seven are mainly small countries – four in Asia, one in Europe, one in South America, and one in Oceania. The table shows the African countries in 2013 according to medical teams, aided facilities, malaria control programs, along with Chinese provinces twinned to each country (Liu, et al. 2014).

The Revolution was important to the presence of the Chinese in Zanzibar. From 1964 onwards the Communist government in China dispatched many teams of experts to Zanzibar. The Chinese consulate has given no official public statements about the aid that China has given to Zanzibar in the last 40 years. There is no doubt that it has been substantial, although in 2004 there were only four teams, one medical team, one team for communications, and two architectural teams, of which one was enlarging the landing strip at the airport(Hsu, 2007).

Traditional Chinese Medicine (TCM) in Tanzania traces its roots back to the 1970s when Chinese doctors accompanied migrant workers and laborers who were working in the construction sites of Tanzania Railway. In addition to these doctors, the Chinese government sent medical doctors to work in hospitals across Tanzania, some of whom decided to settle down and open medical clinics in Dar es Salaam and other urban areas. China earns significant revenue from the production and sales of TCM products worldwide, but especially from malaria-endemic countries like Tanzania, where the prevalence of malaria has created a continuous demand for medication like Artemisinin (Pokam, 2011).

In 2001, Tanzania health officials toured the Chinese medical clinics and confiscated all medicines that were not well packaged or labeled. Although the Tanzania government took an important step in trying to regulate Chinese medicine, the approach of using packaging standards rather than testing for efficacy and safety is also contributing to an increase in fake medicines in the market because packing is all it takes for the medicine to be approved. The Chinese practitioner complained about this intervention as negatively affecting trade, and that the "packaging was not indicative of the medicine's exotic provenance." (Hsu, 2009).

In a speech given on March 31, 2010, Tanzanian President Jakaya Kikwete expressed gratitude for foreign support in building a new cardiac surgery treatment center at Muhimbili National Hospital in Dar es Salaam. The object of president Kikwete's gratitude was neither the United States nor a multilateral institution like the United Nations. Instead, it was China, a country that president Kikwete referred to as "dear rifiki" which in Swahili means "friend" (He, 2012).

Team members were selected by the leadership, he explained, and they came on the grounds of a mutual agreement (Shuang et al.). Most team members were associate professors in (fujiaoshou). One had to have a definite level of technical expertise to be chosen, a definite professional capacity. With one exception that all team members were married; the youngest child was in elementary school level with their spouse in China. Their stay in Zanzibar was not thought to be lucrative. The team members' monthly salary was only marginally higher than in China, but they came here, as their team leader said, to help the 'African' people deal with their diseases. This also allowed them to get to know 'Africa', it was indeed a good opportunity to do so. They knew about 'Africa' through the television. Naturally, it was not as developed as China is now, upon arrival they found conditions more favorable than expected (Hsu 2007).

Hsu (2007) acknowledged some major issues with Acupuncturist stress management in Africa. However, that it would be wrong to fault only the nurses. There were additional problems that made it difficult for patients to get daily treatment: although the treatment was free of charge, public transport to the hospital cost 150 – 200 TS one way, which meant that the patient would have to budget an extra 300 – 400 TS daily for regular treatment, and many patients simply could not afford that. Moreover, the hospital did not have the financial resources to provide for the basics of the treatment. For instance, the skin should be disinfected with a cotton-wool steeped in alcohol before an acupuncture needle is used. Some treatments could be enhanced by charging the needle with low-voltage electricity, but generally, the supply of alcohol and batteries had run out, and patients were required to bring their own for their treatment (which some of the better-off and committed ones did).

Relationship of Chinese Doctors with Tanzanian Local Communities

The disinterest of Chinese doctors to integrate with local communities may suggest that the Chinese doctors are first and foremost passionate, not about using their medical expertise to help the local people, but rather about using the opportunity to work in an African country to further develop their own career goals. I should also note, however, that the relationship between Chinese doctors and African communities may well be driven in part by the government contract for the Chinese doctors. Hsu's research shows that the contract Chinese medical doctors signed before being sent abroad advise them to spend the evening indoors and not mix with the local population outside working hours (Hsu 2007).

Most of them claimed to travel to Tanzania because it is a beautiful country and they want to experience a different life, but these same Chinese doctors have very low interactions with the local people. This may suggest that there is a need for further investigation for the motives of the Chinese personnel in Tanzania and other Sub-Saharan African countries. Because failure to understand the local people's culture may hinder the effective delivery of health care services, the integration of Chinese doctors in these African countries is a component that needs to be addressed (Tesha 2017).

The findings indicate that the Chinese medical personnel in Tanzania provide a variety of health services such as X-ray imaging, CT/MRI scans, physical therapy, consultation, acupuncture, and cupping. Although most of these services are provided in a hospital setting, some are provided in-home settings (Tesha, 2017).

Jennings (2005) concluded that most Chinese health workers do not understand Tanzanian traditional medicine. Most of the participants said that they believe there are advantages and disadvantages in both Tanzania indigenous medicine and Western forms of medicine and that the two can learn from each other. I hypothesized that the Chinese health workers would be critical about the other forms of medicine because they would see them as competitors, but this hypothesis seems to be mistaken. Instead, my findings confirm research that suggests "healing within Tanzania – within Africa – Consists of these multiple agents: coexisting and competing systems all granted legitimacy through use."

South Africa

SAIIA's (South African Institute of International Affairs) 'China in Africa' research project investigates the emerging relationship between China and Africa; analyses China's trade and foreign policy towards the continent; and studies the implications of this strategic co-operation in the political, military, economic and diplomatic fields. The project seeks to develop an understanding of the motives, rationale, and institutional structures guiding China's Africa policy and to study China's growing power and influence so that they will help rather than hinder development in Africa. It further aims to assist African policymakers to recognize the opportunities presented by the Chinese commitment to the continent and presents a platform for a broad discussion about how to facilitate closer cooperation. The key objective is to produce policy-relevant research that allows Africa to reap the benefits of interaction with China, so that a collection and integrated African response to future challenges can be devised that provides for constructive engagement with Chinese partners. A 'China-Africa Toolkit' is being developed to serve

African Policymakers as an information database, a source of capacity building, and a guide to policy formulation (Park, 2009).

The American CDC has many permanent agencies in African countries, and they have played a leading role in the prevention and control of this epidemic. Though various infectious diseases have been effectively controlled in China, the study of tropical diseases and parasitic diseases should not stop China. Moreover, this study needs to be extended to Africa (Lu, 2015). Health in this way is viewed as a tool for promoting economic growth instead of being merely an economic impediment. It becomes a crucial component of broad-based economic and social development, integrated into larger strategies (Youde, 2010).

Interestingly, the second Ministerial Forum of China-Africa Health Development was held in Cape Town, South Africa in October 2015. Its theme was Promoting the Availability of Healthcare Services in Africa in improving China-Africa's Cooperation in Public Health in Post-Ebola Era. There were more than 200 participants, including the health minister of China and over 40 African Countries, as well as representatives from the AU and international organizations such as the World Health Organization and UNAIDS (Tambo, et al. 2016). China's health aid to Africa includes the free provision of Traditional Chinses Medicine (TCM), infrastructural improvement, human resource development cooperation, emergency humanitarian aid, and volunteer programs (Alcorn, 2015, Wenjie 2010).

Figure 2 Geographical Distribution of China's Foreign Aid Funds in 2009The figure of foreign aid written in the white paper report by the Chinese government may seem like a lot, but in comparison to other donors, China's foreign aid is still very low. As can be seen in the comparison chart below, China's development assistance as a share of GNI was less than 0.1%.

The total amount of US$ committed bilaterally (which excludes their donations to multilateral institutions) by the top 10 donors. Limitations of the data notwithstanding, China would rank ninth in bilateral health aid to Africa among bilateral donors, behind the Netherlands but is ahead of Denmark. Since many of the other top-ranked bilateral donor countries are also major multilateral donors, and China has given relatively little to the global health multilateral programs until more recently, this ranking should be interpreted only with regards to bilateral contributions.

Figure 2.

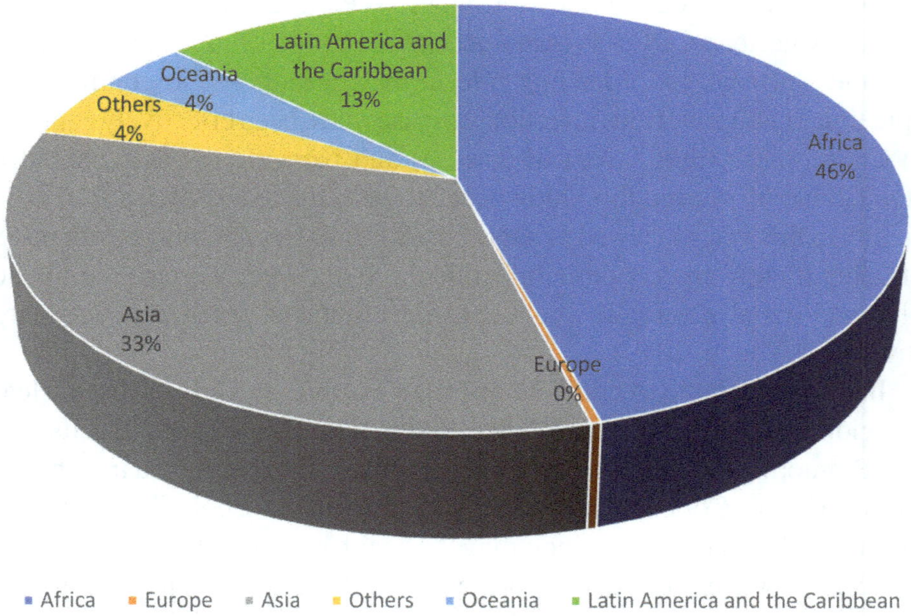

Table 2. Bilateral health aid contributions to Africa, by donors (2000 – 12)

Rank	Donor Country	Commitments to HPWS Projects (USD	Average Annual Contributions (USD million)
1	United States	31,626.50	2,432.80
2	EU Institutions	8,796.80	676.7
3	United Kingdom	6,050.50	465.4
4	France	5,001.09	384.8
5	Germany	4,949.70	380.7
6	Japan	4,456.30	342.8
7	Canada	4,065.40	312.7
8	Netherlands	3,903.70	300.3
9	China	3,029.60	233
10	Denmark	2,200.10	169.2

Source: CAAD (China, in bold and OECD CRS (other donors). Figures refer to only bilateral health aid contributions.

Table 3. Highest Total Commitments to HPWS by African Country (2000 – 12)

Rank	Donor Country	Commitments to HPWS Projects (USD	Average Annual Contributions (USD million)
1	United States	31,626.50	2,432.80
2	EU Institutions	8,796.80	676.7
3	United Kingdom	6,050.50	465.4
4	France	5,001.09	384.8
5	Germany	4,949.70	380.7
6	Japan	4,456.30	342.8
7	Canada	4,065.40	312.7
8	Netherlands	3,903.70	300.3
9	China	3,029.60	233
10	Denmark	2,200.10	169.2

Source: CAAD for China and OECD CRS for other DAC donors. Figures refer to only bilateral contributions, in the case of China, only to Valued Projects.

According to Fan, et al. (2014); Fan Silverman and Grossman (2012) China must consider improving their development activities to support increased aid effectiveness, which could include the use of performance-based financing and improved performance verification, the use of objective criteria to make allocations across countries, and greater experimentation and learning. Imposing health priorities in other countries may have unintended consequences on African's relatively weak health systems. At the very least, an important first step will be to increase the transparency around its health and development related activities in other countries so that recipient countries policymakers alike are better able to track and measure the impact of China's official health financing activities in Africa (Grepin, 2012; Bump et al. 1989).

Multi-sector control effects used in China played an important role in controlling the epidemic in West Africa. This was the first time a Chinese public health training team has worked in West Africa (Lu, 2015).

Figure 3.

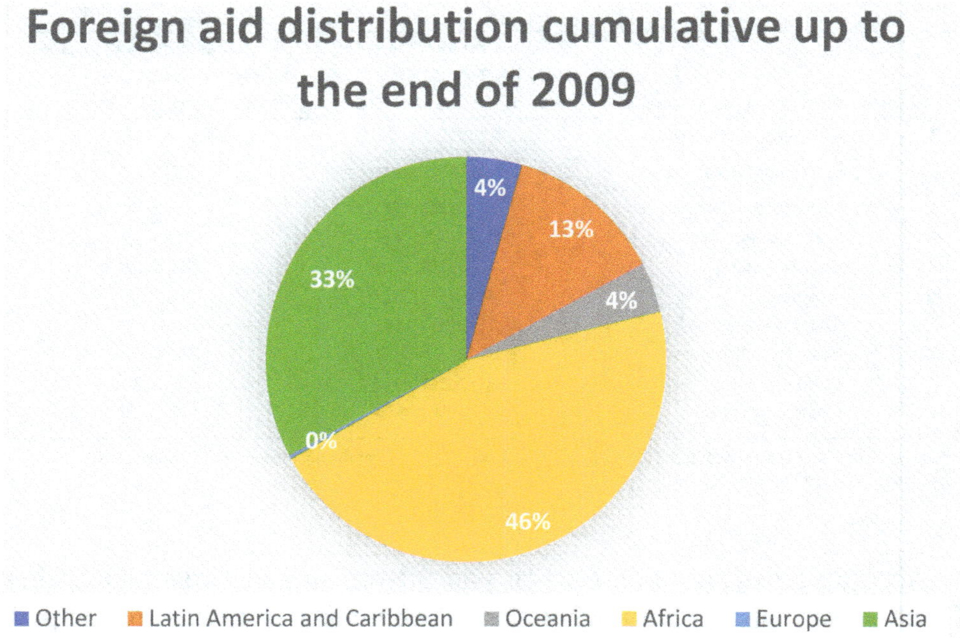

Figure 4.

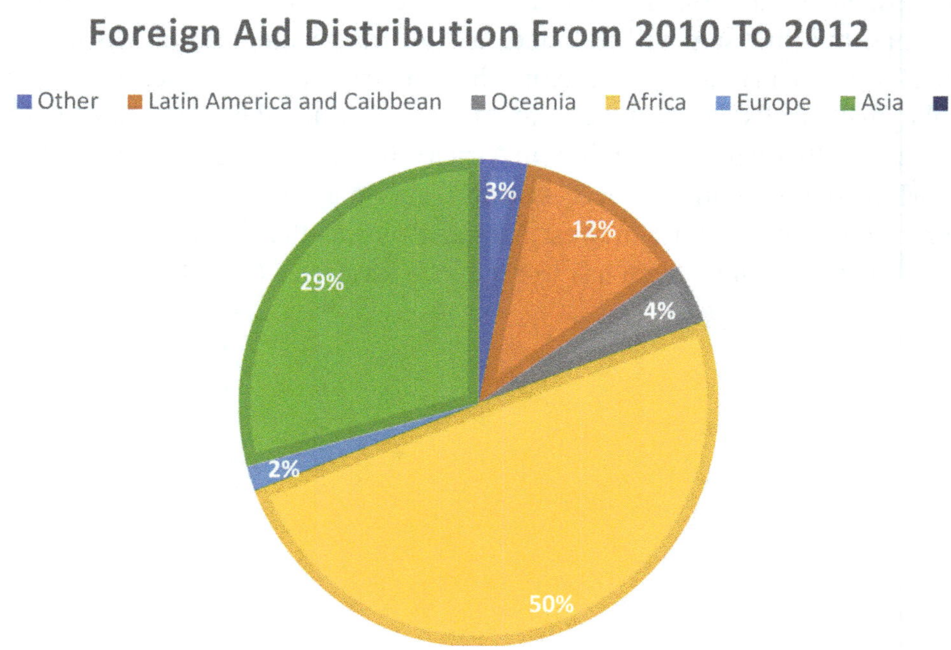

Twinned Chinese Province		China Medical teams			Number of aided facilities	Antimalaria center
		Year Started	Number of up to 2013	Number of members (2013)		
Algeria	Hubei	1963	23	86	0	No
Angola	Sichuan	2009	3	11	2	Yes
Benin	Ningxia	1978	19	26	3	Yes
Botswana	Fujian	1981	13	46	1	No
Burkina Faso	Beijing	1976	10	0	1	No
Burundi	Qinghai	1987	15	29	1	Yes
Cameroon	Shanxi	1974	16	45	6	Yes
Cape Verde	Heilongjiang + Sichuan	1984	15	8	2	No
Central Africa	Zhejiang	1978	15	16	2	Yes
Chad	Jiangxi	1978	10	12	1	Yes
Comoros	Guangxi	1994	9	11	1	Yes
Congo	Tianjin	1967	22	33	4	Yes
Cote d'Ivoire	..	..	..	..	1	Yes
Democratic Republic of the Congo	Hubei	1973	15	18	1	No
Djibouti	Shanxi	1981	17	14	2	No
Egypt	0	..	..	..	0	No
Equatorial Guinea	Guangdong	1971	26	27	1	Yes
Eritrea	Henan	1999	8	18	1	No
Ethiopia	Henan	1974	17	15	1	Yes
Gabon	Tianjin	1977	17	17	2	Yes
The Gambia	Guangdong	1977	9	0	5	No
Ghana	Guangdong	2009	3	11	3	Yes
Guinea	Beijing	1968	23	19	2	Yes
Guinea-Bissau	Guizhou + Sichuan	1976	14	17	4	Yes
Kenya	0	..	..	..	4	Yes
Lesotho	Hubei	1997	9	8	0	No
Liberia	Heilongjiang	1984	7	9	2	Yes
Libya	Beijing	1983	5	0	0	No
Madagascar	Gansu	1975	19	30	1	Yes
Malawi	Shanxi	2008	3	16	0	No
Mali	Zhejiang	1968	23	31	1	Yes
Mauritania	Heilongjiang	1968	30	27	5	No
Mauritius	0	..	..	..	2	No
Morocco	Shanghai	1975	NA*	79	6	No
Mozambique	Sichuan	1976	19	17	0	Yes
Namibia	Zhejiang	1996	9	4	1	No
Niger	Gauangxi	1976	17	37	1	Yes
Nigeria	0	..	..	..	1	Yes
Rwanda	Inner Mongolia	1982	16	20	3	Yes

Table Continues on next page

Twinned Chinese Province		China Medical teams			Number of aided facilities	Antimalaria center
		Year Started	Number of up to 2013	Number of members (2013)		
Sao Tome and Principe	Heilongjiang + Sichuan	1976	11	0	0	No
Senegal	Fujian	1975	15	13	1	Yes
Seychelles	Shandong	1985	14	6	1	No
Sierra Leone	Hunan	1973	16	10	1	Yes
Somalia	Shanghai + Jilin	1965	13	0	2	No
South Africa	0	..	..	..	0	No
South Sudan	Anhui	2012	1	12	1	No
Sudan	Shaanxi	1971	31	42	2	Yes
Swaziland	0	..	..	..	0	No
Tanzania	Shandong + Jiangsu	1964 +1968	48	46	3	Yes
Togo	Shanghai + Shanxi	1974	20	20	2	Yes
Tunisia	Jiangxi	1973	20	45	1	No
Uganda	Yunnan	1983	16	8	1	Yes
Zambia	Henan	1978	16	28	1	Yes
Zimbabwe	Hunan	1985	13	10	3	No
Non-African Countries	NA	NA	66	163	25	No

NA = not applicable. *The number of teams in Morocco is not calculated like other teams so is not presented here. Data sources are shown in the appendix

The American CDC has many permanent agencies in African countries, and they have played a leading role in the prevention and control of this epidemic. Though various infectious diseases have been effectively controlled in China, the study of tropical diseases and parasitic diseases should not stop in China. Moreover, this study needs to be extended to Africa. Chinese-built hospitals have long played an important role in Africa, so existing health care networks should be used to create a disease prevention and control system. After an outbreak of EVD, the Chinese CDC should send personnel abroad. Given these needs, a specialized agency should be created to implement Chinese multi-sector control efforts in foreign countries. The agency should be organized by the Ministry of Health and Family Planning Commission and receive a regular budget so that its effectiveness is ensured (Lu, 2015).

According to the Chinese Health and Family Planning Commission, Minister Li Bin, during 2007 China will provide Africa with "more than 50 training opportunities in healthcare workers". https://ehealthnews.co.za/china-south-african-healthcare

First, when providing medical assistance to Africa, China is affected by political interests. China's government claims that china would not impose any political conditions on recipient countries. However, China suspended all the medical assistance and cooperation and withdrew all the medical teams in the African countries which respectively built formal diplomatic relationships with Taiwan during the 1980s and 1990s, until those countries stopped recognized Taiwan's political status. In those cases, China's medical assistance was related to its interference of the recipient countries' own decisions on the political interactions with Taiwan (Wang and Sun 2014).

Africa is the major beneficiary region of China's foreign aid, but health care is not the most important component of China's foreign aid. Third, the forms of China's foreign aid vary and some of them indeed make contributions to Africa's health care to a different degree, while the others do not (Wang and Sun 2014).

The management of China's medical assistance to Africa is not effective and open enough, and China's medical aid work is not always operating coherently and properly (Wang and Sun 2014).

Some implications could be drawn from the case study of China's medical aid to Africa for the Chinese's overall involvement in global health governance. For instance, China could attach more importance to global health governance, and could learn from the US "Global Health Initiative" and UK's "Health is Global" strategy to formulate and develop a clear, coherent, well-designed strategy or plan for its involvement in global health governance. Besides, solving domestic health care challenges would be beneficial for China's involvement in global health governance, where it could lead by example in more appropriately utilizing the limited health care resources. Moreover, China could explore opportunities to enhance international and multilateral cooperation with other actors to become more comprehensively involved in global health governance (Wang and Sun 2014).

Fifthly, in terms of management of foreign aid, the State Council has nominally the leadership and management rights over China's foreign aid. However, unlike most OECD member states, which have established independent and specialized agencies for foreign aid (eg, USAID, DFID, AUSAID, NORAD, and SIDA), in China, numerous ministries, departments, and bureaus are authorized to partly deal with, or to be responsible for the affairs of assistance – including medical aid to Africa (Wang and Sun, 2014).

Sixthly, in terms of international cooperation, China has been trying to strengthen multilateral and regional cooperation with other aid-providers, such as the Global Fund and the Bill & Miranda Gates Foundation, to provide medical assistance to Africa since 2005 (Wang and Sun, 2014).

Through examining and analyzing the existing literature on China's medical assistance to Africa, as well as conducting a critical analysis of China's only official white paper on its foreign aid, several key findings have been proposed. First, China's medical assistance has a history of 60 years and has notable contributions to the health care sector of Africa. Second, Africa is the major beneficiary region of China's foreign aid, but health care is not the most important component of China's foreign aid. Third, the forms of China's foreign aid vary and some of them indeed make contributions to Africa's health care to a different degree, while the others do not. Fourthly, the management of China's medical assistance to Africa is not effective and open enough, and China's medical aid work is not always operating coherently and properly (Wang and Sun, 2014).

REFERENCES

Brautigam, D. (2009). *The Dragon's Gift: The Real Story of China in Africa.* Oxford University Press.

Bump, J., Fan, V. Y., Lanthorn, H. E., & Yavuz, E. N. (2012). In the Global Fund's court: Experimentation, evaluation, sand the AMFm. *Lancet, 380*(9858), 1989. doi:10.1016/S0140-6736(12)62123-0 PMID:23206836

Da Silva, J. B. Jr, Desiraju, K., Matsoso, P., Minghi, R., & Salagay, O. (2014). BRICS cooperation in strategic health projects. *Bulletin of the World Health Organization, 92*(6), 388–388. doi:10.2471/BLT.14.141051 PMID:24940008

De Prince, P. H. (2011). Chinese Medicine in Cameroon. *China Perspectives, 3*, 51.

Fan, V. Y., Duran, D., Silverman, R., & Glassman, A. (2013). Performance-based financing at the Global Fund: An analysis of grant ratings and funding, 2003 -12. *The Lancet. Global Health, 1*(3), e161–e168. doi:10.1016/S2214-109X(13)70017-2 PMID:25104264

Fan, V. Y., Grepin, K. A., Shen, G. C., & Chen, L. (2014). Tracking the flow of health aid from BRICS countries. *Bulletin of the World Health Organization, 92*(6), 457–458. doi:10.2471/BLT.13.132472 PMID:24940022

Fan, Y.V., Silverman, R., & Glassman, A. (2012). Does HIV/AIDS funding undermine health systems? *Am J Tropic Med Hygiene, 87*(3), 579-580.

Grepin, K. A. (2012). HIV donor funding has both boosted and curbed the delivery of different non- HIV health services in sub-Saharan Africa. *Health Affairs, 31*(7), 1406–1414. doi:10.1377/hlthaff.2012.0279 PMID:22778329

He, T. (2012). *Back to ABCs, Emerging Partnerships among Africa, Brazil, and China*. Academic Press.

Hsu, E. (2007). 2007 Zanzibar, and its Chinese Communities. Institute of social and Cultural Anthology, University of Oxford Popul. *Space Place, 13*(2), 113–124. doi:10.1002/psp.429

Hsu, E. (2009). Chinese propriety medicines: An "Alternative Modernity?" The case of the Anti-Malarial Substance Artemisinin in East Africa. *Medical Anthropology, 28*(2), 111–140. Advance online publication. doi:10.1080/01459740902848303 PMID:19404880

Hsu, E. (2007). *Zanzibar and the Chinese communities: Population, space, and place*. doi:10.1002/psp.429

Jennings, M. (2005). Chinese Medicine and Medical Pluralism in Dar es Salaam: Globalization or Globalisation? *International Relations, 19*(4), 4. doi:10.1177/0047117805058535

Larkin, B. (1970). *China and Africa 1949 – 1970. Berkeley, CA: University of California Press.*

Larkin, B. D. (1975). Chinese Aid in Political Context 1971 -1975. In *Weinstein, Chines, and Soviet Aid.* Academic Press.

Li, A. (2011). *Chinese Medical Cooperation in Africa: With Special Emphasis on the medical Teams and anti-Malaria Campaigns. Discussion paper no. 52*. Nordic African Institute.

Li, A. (2009). Chinese medical teams abroad: a history of medical cooperation. *Foreign Affairs Review, 114*, 25-45.

Liang. (n.d.). *China's Approach in the Blooming South Health Cooperation: Chances, Challenges and the way forward.* Report. China National Health Development Research Center, National Health and Family Planning Commission of the P.R China.

Lin, G., & Reyes, C. Kaufman, & El-Sadr. (2016). *China's health assistance to Africa: opportunism or altruism?* https://globalizationandhealth.biomedcentral.com/articles/10.1186/s12992-016-0217-1

Lin, S. (2016). China's health assistance to Africa: opportunism or altruism? *Globalization and Health, 12*(1). doi:. doi:10118612992-016-0217-1

Liu, P., Guo, Y., Qian, X., Tang, S., Li, Z., & Chen, L. (2014). China's distinctive engagement in global health. *Lancet, 384*(9945), 793–804. doi:10.1016/S0140-6736(14)60725-X PMID:25176550

Liu, P., Guo, Y., Qian, X., Tang, S., Li, Z., & Chen, L. (2014). *China's Distinctive engagement in global health.* www.thelancet.com

Lu, H. (2015). China takes an active role in combating an Ebola outbreak: On-site observations and reflections from a Chinese health care providers. *Intractable & Rare Diseases Research, 4*(4), 217–219. doi:10.5582/irdr.2015.01032 PMID:26668785

McKee, M., Marten, R., Balabanova, D., Watt, N., Huang, Y., Finch, A. P., Fan, V. Y., Van Damme, W., Tediosi, F., & Missoni, E. (2014). BRICS' role in global health and the promotion of universal health coverage: the debate continues. *Bulletin of the World Health Organization, 92*(6), 452–453. doi:10.2471/BLT.13.132563 PMID:24940020

Minghui, R., & Guoping, L. (2014). China's global health strategy. *Lancet, 384*(9945), 719–721. doi:10.1016/S0140-6736(14)61317-9 PMID:25176533

Murray, C. J. L., Anderson, B., Burstein, R., Leach-Kemon, K., Schneider, M., Tardif, A., & Zhang, R. (2011). Development Assistance for health: Trends and prospects. *Lancet, 378*(9785), 8–10. doi:10.1016/S0140-6736(10)62356-2 PMID:21481450

Novotny & Kickbuscz. (2008). Global Health Diplomacy: A bridge to innovative Collaborative Action. *Global Update Forum for Health Research, 5*, 41.

Park, J. Y. (2009). *About China in Africa Project. The South African Institute of International Affairs*. SAIIA.

PLOS ONE. (n.d.). *African Migrant Patients' Trust in Chinese Physicians*. doi:10.1371/journal.pone.0123255.g001

Prasso, S. (2019). China's Digital Silk Road Is Looking More Like an Iron Curtain. *Bloomberg Businessweek*. https://www.bloomberg.com/news/features/2019-01-10/china-s-digital-silk-road-is-looking-more-like-an-iron-curtain

Sridhar, D., Brolan, C. E., Durrani, S., Edge, J., Gostin, L. O., Hill, P., & McKee, M. (2013). Recent Shifts in Global Governance: Implications for the response to Non-communicable Diseases. *PLoS Medicine*.

Sun, Y. (2013). *China in Africa: Implications for US Competition and Diplomacy*. https://www.brookings.edu/research/china-in-africa-implications-for-u-s-competition-and-

Tambo, E., Ugwu, C., Guan, Y., Wei, D., Ning X., & Xiao-Nong, Z. (2016). China-Africa Health Development Initiatives: Benefits and Implications for shaping Innovative and Evidence-informed National Health policies and Programs in Sub-Saharan African Countries. *International Journal Maternal and Child Health AIDS, 5*(2), 119-133.

Tesha, F. (2017). *China's health aid to Africa: An evaluation of China's Health Aid to Africa using a Case Study of Chinese Medicine and Medical Practice in Tanzania*. Academic Press.

Van de Looy, J. (2006). *Africa and China A Strategic Partnership*. Academic Press.

Wang, L., & Bateman, J. (2018). China's Medical Aid in Africa. *The Diplomat*. https://thediplomat.com/2018/03/chinas-medical-aid-in-africa/

Wang, X., & Sun, T. (2014). *China's engagement in global health governance: A critical analysis of China's assistance to the health sector of Africa*. www.jogh.org doi:10.7189/jogh.04.010301

Youde, J. (n.d.). China's Health Diplomacy in Africa. *China an International Journal, 8*(1). Doi:10.1142/S0219747210000099

Chapter 2
Healthcare as a Health Investment

ABSTRACT

This chapter explores healthcare as an investment and the geopolitical implications of healthcare in Africa. The importance of healthcare as a tool of diplomacy is documented and acknowledged. According to Li, the West and China have common interests in Africa regarding economic development and environmental protection. China, Africa, and Western countries must discuss effective methods for increasing cooperation on the continent together. But their interest can sometimes be contradictory in different aspects of the continent. Healthcare is the crossroads of their geo-political implications in Africa. As the PRC evolves from a poor country to a superpower, Africa has become the testing ground for soft power diplomacy via economic development and healthcare.

CHINA HEALTH ASSISTANCE

China has become a major contributor to health assistance in Africa. If China's investments in Africa can be optimally conceptualized and implemented, such resources can substantially contribute to the health and well-being of those in most need in the Africa continent (Lin et al. 2016).

There was a widely held view that most of the rhetoric surrounding China's engagements in Africa has been overblown, particularly the emphasis on negative impacts in terms of internal governance, business and donor

DOI: 10.4018/978-1-7998-4450-1.ch002

practices, and the environment as well as the potential for a major clash with U.S strategic interests. This negative rhetoric is fueled by generalized uncertainty as China's engagement rapidly expands and part by concern about Africa's capacities to manage and shape this engagement to their countries' ultimate benefit (Ishengoma & Bo, 2014).

On Dec 4, Chinese President Xi Jinping revealed US$60 billion in new aid and grants to support development projects in Africa over the next 3 years. The announcement, made at the Forum on China – Africa Cooperation in Johannesburg, South Africa, continued a trend of increased Chinese assistance to the continent, albeit an amount slightly higher than expected. But many observers say the more important question is not how the package is but how it will be spent, and if China's rise can be harnessed to improve public health in Africa in a more durable way (Alcorn, 2015).

Despite the important caveats mentioned above in the valuation of projects, our estimates suggest that China has been pledging health projects valued at USD 231 million a year on average to 46 African countries over the past decade or roughly USD 5 million per country per year. However, Chinese aid appears to be more concentrated than that of more traditional donors: the top 10 recipient countries received 89% of Chinese Health aid to Africa (Murray, et al.2011).

According to Li (2007), the west and China have common interests in Africa regarding economic development and environmental protection, for example. China, Africa, and Western countries must discuss effective methods for increasing cooperation on the continent together. Creating mechanisms of mutual trust and improving dialogue is the best way to prevent potential conflicts between China and the West over Africa. Chinese has used this relationship to develop new goodwill used by the United States to African nations after independence. On the other side, other people see China as a bad will country. They said that China is using a new methodology to scramble African resources. China's increasing presence in Africa has been questioned by several African scholars and social organizations (Konig 2007).

According to Da Silva, et al. (2014) the recent experience with economic development and improved population health, China may have more to offer African Countries than just financial resources. The challenges China historically faced in raising population health status were embedded in the health sector and related sectors, such as agriculture, education, and the environment. The same holds for African Countries today. China has acknowledged these parallels when charting out a long-term vision and financial commitment to partner countries during high-level policy dialogues. Chinese policymakers also believed that such shared experiences deepen their diplomatic relationships with Sub-Saharan African countries. Chinese's engagement in global health is rapidly expanding in other ways beyond the financing of projects in other countries. It has, for example, been a leading player in promoting and supporting inter-BRICS countries initiatives in health (Minghui, et al. 2014; Mckee et al., 2014)

The Chinese Government has a long history of extending health diplomacy to African nations, notable particularly when China was a poor country itself. Beginning in 1963, the country sent teams of doctors, nurses, and health workers on 2-year rotations to provide clinical care in low-resource settings around the world, most of them in Africa. The program continues today with more than 1000 staff deployed abroad at any given time, at an estimated cost of US$60 million annually (Wang 2011; Alcorn, 2015). This shows Chinese is open to a real diplomatic health competition with the western. The only other time they published figures was during the Ebola crisis.

African countries require additional funding to meet the Millennium Development Goals (Soon the Sustainable Development Goals), achieve universal Health Coverage, and other global health priorities, and given that aid flows from traditional donors have plateaued in recent years, there is a need to find new sources of funding for these additional resources (Murray et al., 2011).

Ishengoma and Bo (2014) report said, as a result, the United States sees China as an obstacle to its vision of a developed, liberal, democratic Africa, increasing the likelihood that Washington and Beijing will battle for influence on the continent in the coming years. Chinese economy allowed China to go from being a recipient of foreign aid to establishing itself as a donor nation to African countries.

By 1973, China's foreign aid reached a record high, "the highest when the state's fiscal expenditure of 6% to 7%. China's Selfless assistance did bring some political effect. In 1971, the 26th session of the United Nations General Assembly adopted the overwhelming majority of votes by the Albanian and Algerian countries to restore all the legitimate rights of the People's Republic of China in the United Nations and the deportation of all United Nations agencies. Of the 76 countries that voted in favor of this proposal, 51 were the third world countries of Asia, Africa, and Latin America, the vast majority of which were Chinese foreign aid recipients, which triggered comments such as: "we were carried out by black friends", (Yaping, 2016).

According to Larkins (1975), China and all Africa countries had in common was their shared history and their perception of white dominance by the West. Statements such as "We all belong to the Third World, we are developing countries' were commonly heard at this time. During the conference, China and the African states adopted the five principles of 'Peaceful Coexistence' that had earlier been formulated by India and China. These covered; (1) Mutual respect for sovereignty and territorial integrity; (2) Mutual non-aggression; (3) Non-interference in each other's internal affairs; (4) Equality and mutual benefit; and (5) Peaceful Coexistence.

During the Cold War, tensions between Moscow and Washington grew. China remained independent and focused on other countries instead. In December 1982, the Chinese Premier Zhao Ziyang visited eleven African Countries and promoted the 'Four Principles' of Chinese cooperation with Africa: equality and mutual benefits; an emphasis on practical results; diversity in form; and economic development (Ibid).

In 1989, the events in Tiananmen Square shocked the western world, which questioned the operations of the Chinese government. Third World countries were silent and relations were less affected by the trouble in Beijing. As a result of these events, however, China was forced to focus on old relationships, giving African states a new priority. From then onwards, South-South cooperation was embraced. When official Chinese visits were made to Africa, the main theme was non-interference in each other's affairs. According to one official, 'respect for each other affairs and non-interference should be the basis of the emerging new international order', which referred indirectly to the position that the West takes regarding human rights (Taylor 2005, Van de Looy, 2006).

Lin et al. (2016) discussed a distinctive feature of China's health aid is that is frequently discussed in the literature is what has been referred to as the "no strings attached" altruistic approach which "never imposes ideology, values and development models on other countries, especially African countries". Concerns have been raised regarding this claim indicating that the vision of a democratic Africa where human rights are respected is challenged by China's approach, particularly with its growing influence in the continent. Some have noted that China legitimizes and encourages Africa's most repressive regimes, which leads to enabling weak and failed states. Critics have also expressed concerns that despite its stated approach of "no strings attached", China has its expectations from recipient countries, including diplomatic loyalty on issues such as Taiwan, Tibet, and the status of the Uyghur people.

The action plan agreed upon at the China-Africa Submit stresses the critical need for both sides to enhance communications and cooperation on environmental protection. While a good beginning, concrete steps to implement this are what is needed, which are still absent to date. The interests of the local society must be considered adequately and only through establishing good relations with the African people can win-win results be guaranteed for both Chinese enterprises and local communities. The uses of Chinese labor rather than local workers in Chinese-sponsored projects in Ethiopia, Sudan, and Namibia have been criticized locally (Alden and Davies 2006).

Since China has sought to alleviate the suffering of the Sudanese people with a solution aggregable to all parties, the Sudanese government trusts China. Recently, the Sudanese government has accepted the "hybrid peacekeeping force" in Darfur (Xinhua News, 2007). Konig (2007) stated from different reports express China's investment in Africa as goodwill according to the following phrases; assessing the advantages and disadvantages of Chinese investment in Africa may be simple. A report from the International Journal of Business and Management (Ishengoma & Bo 2014), said that Chinese investments in Africa have been motivated by a desire to access critical resources like oil and bauxite.

According to Alden and Davies (2006), China is believed to contribute to Sudan's civil war. As China's investments in Sudan's oil industry have grown, so too has military cooperation between the two countries. Khartoum is reputed to have spent 80% of the revenue generated by Sudan's oil fields on fighting wars with the country's peripheral regions, including Darfur. Unsurprisingly, the National Congress Party has frequently turned to China for its weapons. China has provided the Sudanese government with Chinese-made tanks, bombers, anti-aircraft guns, helicopters, machine guns, rocket-propelled grenades, and ammunition, all of which were used in the country's long-running civil war.

Sino-African cooperation has played a positive and multifaceted role in Africa. However, China's expanded presence in Africa brings new challenges for China's policies on the continent. China's policies will naturally lag behind the rapidly evolving economic, social, and security environment in Africa, and China will need to adjust accordingly. Although committed to meeting these fluid challenges, China will never waver in its principles of treating Africa with equality, respect, and mutual development (Eiseman, 2005). China also insists on using influence without interference – they view respect as vital to finding solutions. China has used its ties with Sudan to persuade the Sudanese government to cooperate with the United Nations (Chutian, 2007).

According to (Alcorn, 2015) One of the most basic obstacles to improved health and wellbeing in Africa is the high cost of basic drugs and medical supplies, which burdens health systems and limits access for the poorest patients. Some development specialists argue that the Chinese Government has an opportunity to make a longer-lasting contribution to this area. Employing an array of financial instruments, the Chinese Government has spurred joint ventures and technology transfers to other sectors of the African economies, and a policy paper released at the China-Africa Forum indicated that the country would "Encourage Chinese Pharmaceutical enterprises to invest in Africa in a bid to lower the cost of medicine".

The continent's demand for pharmaceuticals is growing faster than almost anywhere else in the world. According to a report by McKensey & Company, between 2010 and 2020, Africa's drug market will expand at five times the rate of the US market and ten times that of Japan, achieving a size of \$40 – 65 billion by the end of the decade. The barriers to entry are equally substantial. The continent is composed of 54 sovereign countries with varied regulatory policies to navigate. There is a dearth of high skilled labor and basic infrastructure, including reliable energy supplies necessary for producing sophisticated goods. The sphere of employment accounted for by the manufacturing sector overall has been declining across much of the region (Alcorn, 2015).

Chinese aid in health is provided in five categories: medical teams, construction of hospitals, donation of drugs and equipment, training of personnel, and malaria control. The largest share of health aid is spent on medical teams and donated facilities. The financial value of Chinese in-kind health aid is difficult to estimate. Crudely, from 2007 – 2011, we estimated the value of Chinese medical teams in Africa to be about \$60 million annually, with donated facilities at a similar amount. Total health aid to Africa annually has been \$150 million. Understanding the type of health support offered rather than the precise volume of funding might be more important. Different from most OECD donors, China does not offer general sectoral support, albeit small cash grants given to several countries in recent years. Its health aid uses a project approach (Liu et, al, 2014).

According to Machaba (2019) state in the World Economic Forum, outlined some major steps to better aid development efficiently. First, we must strengthen our capacity for conducting basic research and clinical trials in Africa. Outside expertise only goes so far, and African policymakers would benefit from more locally derived evidence that helps them better understand which health interventions would be most cost-effective within their country contexts.

Second, the insights gained from these and other initiatives can be translated into effective interventions more quickly through the creation of centers of excellence at the national and regional levels, which can save time and money by propagating the best access solutions and providing guidance on implementation.

Third, we can streamline the approval and procurement of new medicines through secure regulatory harmonization. Developing the regulatory systems needed to ensure access to affordable, quality medicines and other products can be costly and time-consuming, presenting a significant challenge for many African governments. Regulatory harmonization would allow health authorities to validate and make new medicines and health products available across multiple countries using standardized authorization and evaluation criteria.

Fourth, new technologies ranging from data analytics to drones can help tackle supply chain challenges, improving logistical efficiency and eliminating barriers that have historically prevented medicines from reaching remote, underserved populations. New distribution systems, like the partnership Novartis has with Zipline to deliver sickle-cell medicines by drone to rural populations in Ghana, can also bolster security to address the threat of counterfeit medicines – the cause of over 170,000 deaths a year, mostly in Africa.

Fifth, stakeholders must come together to formulate high-level strategies to guide investments in digital technology. A national digital health strategy should set a clear vision for how digital technology will improve healthcare access in a given country; provide clear direction for stakeholders across the health system; and establish a supportive, predictable operating environment for solution providers. A 2017 report from the Broadband Commission provides useful guidance on the cross-sector collaboration essential for effective national digital health strategies.

Holst (2019) recognized that Sub-Saharan Africa has become an emerging arena for digital health innovations directed at strengthening health care, in terms of both patient management and disease surveillance and prevention. Across the region with the world's largest burden of disease and the most severe shortage of health-care workers, we see increased use of digital health solutions and interventions for clients, health-care providers, health-system managers, and data services. As the traditional health-care systems are typically ill-equipped, understaffed, or not accessible at all, sub-Saharan Africa is booming with digital health.

Prasso (2019) A large number of Chinese investments and digital technologies are pouring into the African continent. Zambia is spending USD 1 billion on China-built surveillance, telecommunications, and broadcasting equipment. Roy (2019) The topic of China's expanding digital infrastructure is often understated. The digital aspect of the Belt Road Initiative (BRI) should be the most weighted issue especially for African states that are still in the preliminary stages of building digital infrastructure as it could generate security concerns in the foreseeable future.

China has also been promoting the use of Beidou which is often called the "digital glue" that would weave all Chinese technologies into a single thread. (Wall Street, 2016) Beidou is an alternative to the US's Global Positioning System (GPS) system and will most likely become an "essential" for smartphone users across the BRI economies. The Chinese are already strategical ahead of the west in digital support to Africa. Roy (2019) argues Africa should learn to leverage the technologies and infrastructure provided by China and aim to build and promote their indigenous digital ecosystem. This integrated approach of Africa would give them more bargaining power over China and other players.

In the period 2006 – 2007, the Organization for Economic Cooperation and Development's Development Assistance Committee (DAC) members committed an average of 18 percent of their bilateral sector aid to health; the largest donor – the United States – allocated 28 percent. The Obama administration's HIV/AIDS funding absorbed 70 percent of US health-related development aid (Dugger, 2009). In 2010, the United States budgeted $8 billion in aid for sub-Saharan Africa; global health and child survival came to $4.7 billion (57 percent). The top five recipients of US bilateral health assistance in sub-Saharan Africa in the fiscal year 2012 were projected to be Kenya ($545 million), South Africa ($510 million), Nigeria (471 million), Tanzania (346 million), and Uganda (323 million) (USAID 2012).

In recent years the Chinese have linked their aid funding announcements to the United Nations summits on financing the Millennium Development Goals (MDCs) and meetings of the Forum on China-Africa Cooperation (FOCAC). Most commitments are made in increasingly specific quantities rather than money amounts (Global Health Initiative 2012). Contrary, to the United States, seeing China as an obstacle to its vision of a developed, liberal, democratic Africa, increasing the likelihood that Washington and Beijing will battle for influence on the continent in the coming years. Chinese economy allowed China to go from being a recipient of foreign aid to establishing itself as a donor nation to African countries (Ishengoma and Bo, 2014).

Since 1963, under the protocol on the dispatch of medical teams signed between the government of China and the recipient countries, about 23,000 Chinese medical workers have been sent to 66 countries to provide services to an estimated 270 million people. At the end of 2013, 1171 Chinese medical workers were working in 113 medical centers in 49 countries. 42 of these countries are in Africa, and the remaining seven are mainly small countries – four in Asia, one in Europe, one in South America, and one in Oceania (Liu, et al. 2014).

The largest and most powerful African countries such as South Africa, Nigeria, and Kenya do not have Chinese medical teams. Chinese selection of hosting countries is based on country request and the joint decision by China's Ministries of Health, foreign affairs, and finance. The medical team is overseen by the Chinese embassy's economic and commercial counselor's offices (Liu et. al., 2019).

But there are several reasons why the Chinese Government could be poised to promote joint ventures with African companies and change this dynamic where other parties have not. One is that Chinese firms can capitalize on the vertical integration with supplies of active pharmaceutical ingredients in their home country. Prashant Yadav, a senior fellow at the University of Michigan's William Davidson Institute, USA, says that small African manufacturers often struggle to pay upfront for their supplies, sometimes as much as 6 months of future revenue (Alcorn, 2015).

Unfortunately, there is a paucity of information regarding the scale, scope, and impact of Chinese health aid to Africa. Irrespective of the nature of the assistance, there is a need for a systematic and rigorous evaluation of the various approaches and investments. Such assessments could be critical in informing future investments and consequently serving to advance the health of the target populations (Lin, 2016)

Finally, there is a need for African leaders, who are passionate about positive change and who represent African communities, to be actively and fairly involved in the determination and rigorous evaluation of the various elements of China's health aid to African countries. This, I argue, will enable all parties involved to gain a deeper understanding of how the priorities and allocations for health aid are determined, how much aid fits within the specific African Country's health strategies, and finding efficient means to assess the terms, implementation, and effectiveness of such aid (Lin, 2016).

REFERENCES

Alcorn, T. (2015). *New orientation for China's health assistance to Africa*. Academic Press.

Alden, C., & Davies, M. (2006). A profile of the operations of Chinese multinationals in Africa. *South Africa Journal of International Affairs*, *13*(1), 83–96. doi:10.1080/10220460609556787

China's 'One Belt, One Road' Takes to Space. (2016, Dec. 28). *The Wall Street Journal*. https://blogs.wsj.com/chinarealtime/2016/12/28/chinas-one-belt-one-road-takes-to-space/

Chutian Metropolis Daily. (2007). *What Kind of Issue Darfur Is: A Special Interview with the Special Representative of the Chinese Government*. Author.

Da Silva, J. B. Jr, Desiraju, K., Matsoso, P., Minghi, R., & Salagay, O. (2014). BRICS cooperation in strategic health projects. *Bulletin of the World Health Organization*, *92*, 388–388.

Dugger, C. W. (2009, Oct. 30). As Donors Focus on AIDS, Child Illnesses Languish. *New York Times*.

Eisenman, J. (2005, July 5). Zimbabwe: China's African Ally. *China Brief*, *5*(15), 9–11.

Giry, S. (2005). *China's Africa Strategy*. https://www.cfr.org/publication/8436/chinas_rising_role_in_africa.html

Global Health Initiative. (n.d.). http://foreifnassistance.gov/initiative_GH_2012.aspx?FY=2012

Holst, C., Sukum, F., Radavnovic, A., Ngowi, B., Noll, J., & Winkler, A. (2020). Sub-Sahara Africa-The new bleed ground for a global digital health. *Lancet*. doi:10.1016/S2589-7500(20)30027-3

Ishengoma, H. J., & Bo, S. (2014). To discuss Different Reports about Chinese Investment in Africa and CIF. *Journal Mass Communication & Journal*, *4*, 8. doi:10.4172/2165-7912.10000214

Konings, P. (2007). China and Africa: Building a strategic partnership. *Journal of Developing Societies*, *23*, 341–367.

Larkin, B. D. (1975). Chinese Aid in Political Context 1971 – 1975. In *Weinstein, Chinese and Soviet Aid*. Academic Press.

Machaba, P. (2017). *How to start a digital healthcare revolution in Africa in 6 steps*. Retrieved, May 22, 2020, from https://www.weforum.org/agenda/2019/08/6-ways-digital-technology-can-transform-healthcare-in-africa/

McKee, M., Marten, R., Balalanova, D., Watt, N., Huang, Y., Finch, A., Fan, V. Y., Van Damme, W., & Tediosi Missoni, F. (2014). E: BRICS' role in global health and the promotion of universal health coverage: the debate continues. *Bulletin of the World Health Organization*, *92*, 452–453.

Minghui, R., & Guoping, L. (2014). China's global health strategy. *Lancet*, *384*, 719–721.

Mohon, S., Xu, J., Jing, J., King, M., Zhang, J., Wang, P., Bouey, J., & Cheng, F. (2017). China's engagement with Development assistance for health in Africa. *Global Health Research and Policy*, *2*(24).

Roy, K. (2019). *Deciphering Beijing's digital connection in Africa*. Retrieved, May 20, 2020, From https://idsa.in/africatrends/beijing-digital-connection-in-africa-kroy#footnote4_pfdiym1

USAID. (2012). *Congressional Budget Justifications, Foreign Operations, Annex on Regional Operations, Budget Year 2012*. https://www.usaid.gov/performance/cbj/158268.pdf

Van de Looy, J. (2005). *Africa and China a Strategic Partnership*. African Studies Centre. ASC Working Paper 67/2006.

What Kind the Darfur Issue Is: a special interview with the special representative of the Chinese government. (2007, July 8). *Chutian Metropolis Daily*.

Xinhua. (2007). Sudan government deals with Darfur with a light pack. *News Agency*. Retrieved, May 23, 2020 from http://news.xinhuanet.com/world/2007-07/15/content_6377969.htm

YapingQ. (2011). *60 7%*. http://history.people.com.cn/GB/205396/14757191.html.2

Chapter 3
Current Healthcare Collaborative Projects in Africa Between the USA and the PRC

ABSTRACT

African public healthcare systems suffer from a significant "brain drain" of their healthcare professionals and knowledge. As health workers migrate to wealthier countries such as Australia, Canada, the USA, and the United Kingdom, Africa is struggling to meet its healthcare needs. PRC is playing an increasingly important role in the African public health sector. However, only a handful of countries have received priority in receiving Chinese development assistance for healthcare. The USA has struggled with the development of new strategies for international development. As the USA has been reducing healthcare options in the developing nations in Africa, PRC has increased money and expertise for Africa.

INTRODUCTION

China is playing an increasingly important role in the African public health sector. However, only a handful of countries have received priority in receiving Chinese development assistance for health. The findings from our study confirm that: China is engaged in helping African countries to develop their health systems by helping develop infrastructure and supplying equipment and medicine, as well as training health professionals and funding disease

DOI: 10.4018/978-1-7998-4450-1.ch003

treatment. However, very limited attention has been paid to addressing disease prevention, health education, and health promotion and awareness. Furthermore, financial sustainability and the involvement of NGOs and the private sector has been relatively ignored, which raises questions regarding the long-term sustainability and impact that Chinese health aid projects can have in Africa ((Shajalal et al., 2017).

BACKGROUND

African public health care systems suffer from a significant "brain drain" of their health care professionals and knowledge as health workers migrate to wealthier countries such as Australia, Canada, the USA, and the United Kingdom. Knowledge generated on the continent is not readily accessible to potential users on the continent. In this paper, the brain drain is defined as both a loss of health workers (hard brain drain) and unavailability of research results to users in Africa (soft brain drain) ((Muula, 2005, p. 21-29). Inshigan and Bo 2014 concluded Chinese relations with African countries have been positive in some ways. Unfortunately, many African leaders have embraced the Chinese model allowing them to maintain a struggle grip on political power.

In recent decades, China's presence in African countries has become more prominent. Through the China- Africa collaboration, significant events have occurred in Africa's infrastructures, oil and gas, technical cooperation, human resource development, agriculture, real estate, humanitarian aid, and health assistance programs. As shown in figure 1, China has invested in many different sectors to promote the growth of Africa. While China's ministry of health plays a technical role in healthcare, one of the most critical components to the China- Africa collaboration still lies in the healthcare system. Healthcare in Africa is an intricate and multidimensional subject that requires a broad perspective to fully comprehend its components which include vaccines, pharmaceuticals, hospitals, medical technology, supplies, and human resources.

Figure 1. Chinese investment in Africa

Note. Figures of the week: Chinese investment in Africa, Sow, M. (2018, September 6). Figures of the week: Chinese investment in Africa. Brookings. https://www.brookings.edu/blog/africa-in-focus/2018/09/06/figures-of-the-week-chinese-investment-in-africa/

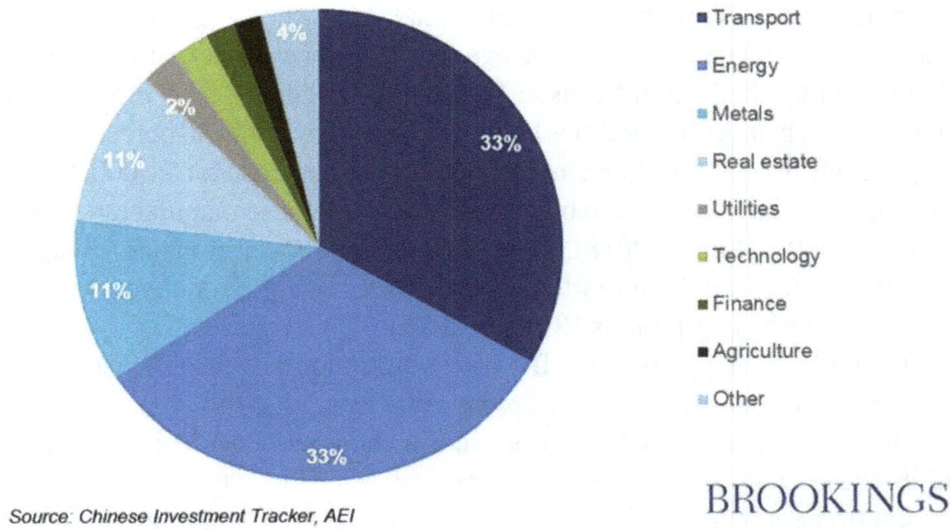

Vaccine/Pharmaceuticals

At the first Ministerial Conference for the Forum on China-Africa Cooperation (FOCAC), President Xi Jinping announced the Beijing Declaration of the China-Africa Health Development (Alcorn, 2015, p. 2379-2380). The Beijing Declaration of the China-Africa Health Development which took place from 10 to 12 October 2000 identified several health issues that will be targeted in Nigeria and other African countries. Some of the targeted health concerns include HIV/AIDS, malaria, schistosomiasis, reproductive health, immunization, and vaccine-preventable diseases.

Improving the healthcare system in Africa requires a multifaceted approach, however, one of the fundamental obstacles limiting Africa's health system is the high cost of drugs. The lack of access to affordable drugs factors tremendously into the quality of health for those living in poverty. By strategically utilizing financial resources and technology, China has encouraged Chinese pharmaceutical enterprises such as Guilin to invest in Africa at a more affordable price. Guilin has developed branches in Ghana, Nigeria, and Côte d'Ivoire and regional offices in five other African countries (Alcorn, 2015, p. 2379-2380). For now, these countries dispense imported drugs rather than manufacturing them themselves (Alcorn, 2015, p. 2379-2380). However, Vice-president Lily Su suggested that Guilin has plans to establish manufacturing companies in Africa (Alcorn, 2015, p. 2379-2380).

A few African countries have welcomed Chinese investments in pharmaceuticals with the hopes of enhancing access to cost-effective medication to the public. These changes are already evident in Tanzania, as highlighted by the Health Minister Ummy Ali Mwalimu, who reports that "The price of health commodities has been reduced by about 40 percent…For example, we used to buy some medicine, let's say one dose for $1,000. Right now, since we have decided to buy directly from Chinese manufacturers, we get it for $600" (Ruinan, 2018). The China-Africa cooperation has reshaped the delivery method for imported drugs by decreasing the delivery period from 6-9 months to 3 months (Ruinan, 2018).

Despite these improvements, Africa seeks to develop its local pharmaceutical manufacturing industries and I implore them to pursue this. Less than 2% of drugs utilized in Africa are produced in the continent (Ruinan, 2018). Additionally, Ummy Ali Mwalimu revealed that "imports account for 85 percent of the pharmaceutical products in Ethiopia. In Kenya, a country that has the most developed pharmaceutical local manufacturing industry in East Africa, import dependency still stands above 70 percent." (Ruinan, 2018). As shown in figure 2, the rates of China importing to Africa have drastically increased since 2002.

The United Nations (UN) revealed that by 2050, Africa's population is expected to more than double due to rapid urbanization rates and fertility rates. This demographical transition in addition to the economic development will require investments in pharmaceuticals and other health commodities (Ruinan, 2018). However, the obstacle delaying this shift for Africa is the high dependency on imports. Although Africa's dependency on China seems to juxtapose the hope for independent pharmaceuticals in Africa, Jane Xing, deputy director of the Bill & Melinda Gates Foundation China Office suggest that China can play a vital role and cooperate with African countries to help develop its own effective and efficient pharmaceutical industry." (Ruinan, 2018). Granting, these plans are still in the works, but hopefully, there will be distinct changes in Africa's pharmaceutical system.

Figure 2. China's importing and exporting growth in Africa
Note. Data: China-Africa trade — China Africa research initiative. (n.d.). China Africa Research Initiative. https://www.sais-cari.org/data-china-africa-trade

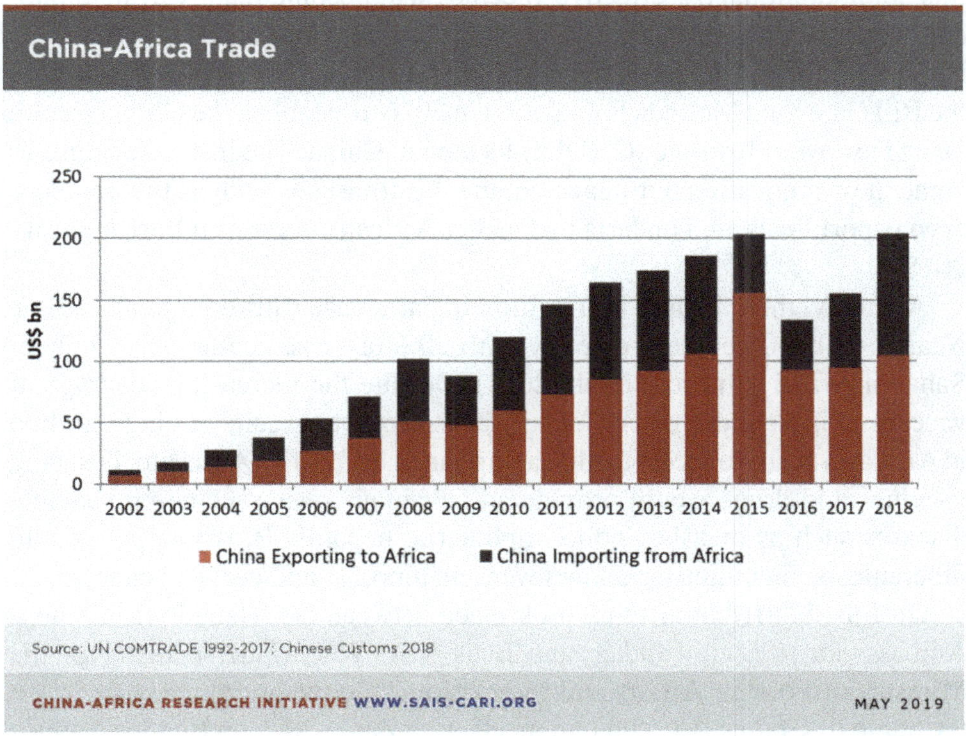

Vaccines

According to (Zheng et al., 2018), China has one of the world's largest vaccine industries. Annually, China produces approximately 700 million vaccine doses (Zheng et al., 2018).

"China is currently producing nearly all of the commonly-used vaccines for viral diseases such as influenza, measles, rabies (for humans), mumps, rotavirus, hepatitis A and B and bacterial diseases, including typhoid, tetanus, and diphtheria," states Dr. Xu Ming, Vice President of the China Chamber of Commerce for Import and Export of Medicines and Health Products ("China enters the global vaccine market," 2014, p. 626-627).

Chinas partnership with Africa's healthcare system encompasses different sectors including the production and distribution of vaccines. China Merchants Charitable Foundation (CMCF), a group associated with the charity foundation China Merchants Group (CMG), has committed $1.5

million US dollars to Gavi, the Vaccine Alliance, to aid developing countries with childhood immunization ("Gavi, the Vaccine Alliance", 2017) Through this collaboration, cost-effective vaccines will become readily available for children in Africa and Asia (Gavi, The Vaccine Alliance, 2017). Also, the Beijing Municipal Government and Tsinghua University joined efforts with the Bill Gates and Melinda Foundation in 2016 to establish the Global Health Drug Discovery Institute (GHDDI) located in China. The institution aims to create new innovational drugs to combat health issues such as tuberculosis, cryptosporidiosis, and malaria that afflict African countries (Olbrich & Lili, 2018).

Annually, there is over 200 million malaria case (Strydom et al., 2014). Nearly, 600,000 people die yearly with 90% of these deaths occur in sub-Saharan Africa (Strydom et al., 2014). Despite the increasing coverage of vaccines,1 in 5 children in Africa still lacks access to vaccines (1 in 5 children in Africa do not have access to life-saving vaccines," 2017). Access to lifesaving vaccines and drugs would provide an advantage over vaccine-preventable diseases such as measles, polio, diphtheria, hepatitis B, whooping cough, tuberculosis, meningitis, yellow fever, pneumonia, and cervical cancers.

On July 5, 2018, a meeting took place between He Xiangdong, Chinese Ambassador to South Sudan, and Baak V.A. Wol, Undersecretary of the Ministry of Foreign Affairs and International Cooperation of South Sudan ("Charge d'Affaires A.i. Zhu Qin meets with Zanny Minton Beddoes, editor of the economist," 2018). Both parties signed an agreement for China to donate anti-malaria drugs worth 5 million RMB Yuan, medical supplies valued at 20 million RMB Yuan and an additional 1 million US dollars cash donation to the South Sudanese government ("Charge d'Affaires A.i. Zhu Qin meets with Zanny Minton Beddoes, editor of the economist," 2018). These donations were given in hopes of improving South Sudan's healthcare system and control infectious diseases such as malaria and rift valley fever ("Charge d'Affaires A.i. Zhu Qin meets with Zanny Minton Beddoes, editor of the economist," 2018).

The timeline of this agreement coincided with the needs of South Sudan. In 2018, the United States administration announced its punitive and comprehensive reevaluation of humanitarian aid to South Sudanese. (Sen, 2018) According to the Trump Administration, the South Sudanese government has

"Squandered this partnership [with the United States], pilfered the wealth of South Sudan, killed their people, and repeatedly demonstrated their inability and unwillingness to live up to their commitments to end the country's civil war. The result is one of Africa's worst humanitarian disasters. The Government of South Sudan has lost credibility, and the United States is losing patience," (Sen, 2018)

From a humanitarian perspective, withdrawing aid from an underdeveloped country as a form of punishment to the government is counterproductive because the civilians are the ones that will suffer. Doing so could plunge South Sudan further into disaster. The U.S. is one of the biggest donors in South Sudan providing more than $3 billion in aid to the South Sudan Humanitarian Response Plan (SSHRP) since 2011.'913) Using these funds, "Almost 3 million people received emergency health kits, and nearly one million children and pregnant and lactating women were treated for malnutrition" (Yayboke, 2018) The lack of funds would endanger the lives of 7.6 million people in need of aid. However, in light of the United states re-evaluating its financial support to the South Sudanese government, it has created an opportunity for China to further establish itself in South Sudan as a primary influence in the future stability and economic viability by investing wisely in healthcare, humanitarian aid, infrastructures, and the oil industry.

Hospitals/ Infrastructures

One of the many objectives of the China-Africa co-operation on health is to establish 100 hospitals and clinics in Africa. (Skosana, 2015) Over the years, China has taken tremendous effort to fulfill this commitment and has been consistent in establishing numerous amounts of hospitals throughout Africa and creating access to medical facilities and primary care. Deborah Brautigam, director of the China-Africa Research Initiative at Johns Hopkins University School of Advanced International Studies, Washington, DC, USA, has encountered Chinese-built facilities in Ethiopia, Zambia, and Sierra Leone. Although the buildings are often needed, she observes they are not well integrated into the local health system countries (Alcorn, 2015, p. 2379-2380).

In 2015, China-funded Niger with 66 million US dollars to construct the largest and most modern referral hospital in West Africa, now known as Niamey General Referral Hospital (Murielle, 2016). The hospital offers all medical services including radiology, cardiology, emergency medicine, psychiatry, and neurosurgery services (Murielle, 2016). Within the hospital houses over 500 beds and was constructed on 16 hectares of land by China Geo-Engineering Corporation (CGC) (Murielle, 2016) Moreover, the hospital consists of an outpatient building with wheelchair ramps, an emergency building, a medical technology building, and a public hall. Also, there are laboratories, blood banks, and 16 surgical rooms. (Murielle, 2016).

Figure 3. Gallery of General Hospital of Niger
Note. General Hospital of Niger / CADI. (2016, October 30). ArchDaily. https://www.archdaily.com/798313/general-hospital-of-niger-cadi

Niger

Access to healthcare in Niger is a multi-dimensional issue that encompasses several determining factors such as transportation, financial availability, geographical availability, and physical availability. According to the World Bank, Niger is one of the poorest countries (The World Bank, n.d.). On the United Nations Human Development Index, Niger ranks 187th out of 188 countries (The World Bank, n.d.). Furthermore, Niger's exposure to the dry and wet seasons increases the prevalence of diseases such as malaria, measles, meningitis, polio and pneumonia, and Cholera (Blanford et al., 2012, p. 24). Besides, access to care is limited during these critical periods because small clinics experience shortages in medical staff, resources, medical equipment, and facilities to adequately treat and monitor the large influx of patients (Blanford et al., 2012, p. 24).

However, access to medications and vaccinations could improve these health disparities and decrease the rates of communicable diseases. Niamey

General Referral Hospital is located in the heart of the country and this essential factor will provide access to the public which can improve the time traveled to receive medical attention.

Zambia

Levy Mwanawasa General Hospital, located in Zambia, is another hospital funded by the Chinese government and built by a Chinese company, Shanxi Construction Engineering Group (Smith, 2013) In August 2011, China helped Zambia to establish its first general hospital in Lusaka, which reduced the strain on the century-old University Teaching hospital that has existed as the largest hospital in Zambia (Smith, 2013)

The hospital was composed of 159 beds, births an average of 260 babies per month, and attends to an estimated 2,600 patients (Smith, 2013) The hospital includes dental and maternity wards as well as laboratories. According to China daily, Zambia's medical services and hospital system will become similar to China's very own national three-tier medical assessment system (杨洋, 2017). Chinese Embassy charge d' affaires, Chen Shijie provided further support of the project stating "I believe that there is a great potential of medical co-operation between China and Zambia. More Chinese medical equipment and medicine will be accessible to the Zambian market which will help to alleviate the shortage of medicines in the country (Charles Chisala, 2017).

Following the launch of Levy Mwanawasa General Hospital in 2011, another phase of construction began. On June 7th, 2017, Mr. Edgar Chagwa Lungu, President of the Republic of Zambia alongside Mr.Wang Young, State Councillor Peoples Republic of China announced phase II of the Levy Mwanawasa General Hospital (Ngosa, 2019). The hospital would be transformed from a general hospital to a teaching hospital to broaden medical services to provide quality health care in Zambia and to cultivate a learning environment for future Zambian health professionals (Ngosa, 2019). This monumental change will not only establish Levy Mwanawasa Medical University (LMMU) as the first leading Public Medical University in Zambia, but it will transcend medical training in a positive direction that will hopefully revolutionize healthcare in Zambia (Ngosa, 2019).

To address the admirable work the 19th Chinese medical had accomplished during the southern African nation tour, Zambia's Minister of Health, Chitalu Chilufya awarded an honorary certificate to Qi Zuhong, the team leader, Chinese embassy officials, and the 28 individuals on the medical team in

Lusaka, Zambia, on May 14, 2018 (Xinhua, 2018). During their tour, the 19th Chinese medical team provided training to high-level medical staff in Zambia through "clinical teaching, academic lectures, and mutual expert visits" which incorporated traditional Chinese medical treatment methods and medical (Xinhua, 2018). Qi Zuhong reported that by the end of their tour in April 2018, his team had treated 15,275 patients, saved 392 critically ill patients, and performed 726 surgical operations and 3,080 anesthesia operations (Xinhua, 2018). Also, the team assisted in training 352 local medical employees and donated over 120,000 U.S. dollars for medical equipment and (Xinhua, 2018). Since China's presence in the 1990s, they have sent 515 physicians to Zambia and continue to provide resources to help develop the health care sector (Xinhua, 2018).

Uganda

In 2012, the Chinese government donated the China-Uganda Friendship Naguru Hospital worth US 8 million as a gift to the Uganda government. The hospital provides free specialized health services to the public (Administrator Ministry of health, 2020). Naguru Hospital offers inpatient services, outpatient services, specialized curative care services, diagnostic services prevention and rehabilitation, community outreach services, management, and support services (Administrator Ministry of health, 2020). Since the opening of Naguru hospital in 2012, the patient volume has increased tremendously, and most of the population receive services for reproductive health, urology, gastroenterology, orthopedics, acupuncture, E.N.T, diabetes, hypertension, and specialized pediatrics (Administrator Ministry of health, 2020).

This hospital serves as a dynamic change in Uganda's healthcare system because it reduces the influx of patients to Mulago National Referral Hospital. Before the establishment of China-Uganda Friendship, Naguru Hospital, Mulago National Referral Hospital was the only general hospital attending to an estimated population of 3 million people (Administrator Ministry of health, 2020). AfricaNews acknowledged China's impact on Uganda stating "Uganda's healthcare system is improving thanks to hospital and medical equipment donated to the country by China"(AfricaNews, 2018). More notably, the doctors testified that maternal deaths in the hospital have declined by 99%" (AfricaNews, 2018). "We can operate over 7,000 [patients], deliver over 22,000 mothers [annually] and in so doing we can have over 99.7 percent of them going back home alive and better than they came in," said Emmanuel

Batiibwe, director of the hospital (AfricaNews, 2018). Maternal mortality rates are highest in sub-Saharan Africa. However, the Uganda Demographic and Health Survey (UDHS) revealed a decline in maternal mortality rates (Apolot et al., 2019). The rates have decreased from 438 deaths in 2011 to 336 deaths per 100,000 live births in 2017 (Apolot et al., 2019).

Ethiopia

In Ethiopia, China supported the launch of Tirunesh Beijing General Hospital (TBGH) (Tadesse, 2017). The hospital cost $12.7 million and opened in 2012. TBGH provides access to outpatient, inpatient, and emergency services to citizens in the Akaki-Kality sub-city, towns by the Oromia regional State area, and the Addis Ababa region (Tadesse, 2017). Chinese medical professionals from the Henan Province are also stationed at the hospital to contribute their expertise (Tadesse, 2017). In August 2017, the hospital expanded and added two new departments the Emergency and Trauma Treatment Center and Maternal and Child Health Care Center (Tadesse, 2017). From La Yifan's perspective, the Chinese Ambassador to Ethiopia

"Improving the health industry will not only improve the basic healthcare service of Ethiopia, but it will also improve the investment climate. The healthcare system is one of the basic elements considered when they [the Ethiopian Government] make decisions." (Tadesse, 2017).

One of the primary health challenges Ethiopia faces are non-communicable diseases (NCD) such as malaria, tuberculosis, and HIV/AIDS. As the rates of NCD continue to increase there will be a demand for health commodities such as clinics and hospitals. Tirunesh-Beijing Hospital helps fill this role by reducing the gap between communicable and non-communicable diseases. Furthermore, Tirunesh-Beijing Hospital has enabled an extensive collaboration in medicine which has resulted in an exchange in strategic intervention plans and medical practices such as acupuncture (Tadesse, 2017). Acupuncture, also known as the "magic doctor" and "deity needle" by the locals' functions as an alternative holistic treatment. (Tadesse, 2017).

Medical Supplies/ Technology

Over recent decades, technology has played a vital role in the development of the human race. More specifically, technology has played an innovative role in medicine, pharmaceuticals, healthcare, and medical informatics. Because of its multidimensionality, medical technology and medical supplies are a focal point in the China-Africa healthcare collaboration.

According to the UN, 50-80% of medical supplies in developing countries are not operating (Moyimane et al., 2017) This critical challenge creates a barrier in healthcare because it prevents effective diagnosis, monitoring, and quality of care. The healthcare initiative highlighted the critical need for medical supplies, mobile medical services, and advanced diagnostic equipment.

Namibia

An innovative change in medical technology is already evident in the Brightness Action Program in Namibia which was launched in 2018. The program aims to treat eye diseases. As part of the program, the Chinese government donated medical supplies worth 279,000 U.S. dollars for cataracts surgeries (Xinhua, 2018). This new equipment will allow Namibia's health ministry to provide free cataract surgeries to 200 patients in the rural area of Windhoek and Rundu (Xinhua, 2018). This opportunity for cataracts surgery provides hope for the 10,450 estimated individuals that are critically impaired and need surgery. In addition to the supplies, Chinese surgical teams worked with the staff at Windhoek Central Hospital which helped alleviate the shortage of medical staff. Helena Ndume, the Director of the Ophthalmology Department at Windhoek Central Hospital provided positive feedback concerning the program stating

You can see here, there are so many many patients, we have been doing this for many years, but still, we can't finish them (the treatments) because we don't have many doctors, so we are very happy that the people from China have come to help us, to fight this preventable blindness caused by cataracts, we are very very fortunate, and we hope they can come again (Xinhua, 2017).

Another innovative use of technology, known as Telemedicine, allows physicians to examine a patient remotely. This remote consultation provides access to Healthcare for individuals dwelling in rural areas, people with limited medical personnel, or patients with chronic diseases. Although telemedicine has its challenges such as internet connectivity, this novel platform has established an international collaboration between African and Chinese medical physicians.

In 2017, the Smart Health System was launched by the African Union (AU) and ZTE, which is one of China's multinational telecommunication cooperation. The Smart Health system created an integrated electronic medical record system and established telemedicine between China and Ethiopia (Xinhua, 2017). The Henan Provincial People's Hospital, located in China, assembled a virtual consultation center in Ethiopian Black Lion Hospital to aid with the scarcity of pathology specialists in Ethiopia (Mei, 2018).

On March 21, 2017, the 18th Chinese Medical Team in Zambia donated 3 telemedicine devices which will be installed at the University Teaching Hospital in Lusaka, Livingstone Hospital, and Ndola Hospital. ("Chinese medical team donates more telemedicine equipment to Zambian hospitals," 2017). Before this, the first telemedicine device was set up at the Levy Mwanawasa Hospital in Lusaka. Dr. Jianjun Guo, the team leader of the 18th medical team in Zambia, reported that the telemedicine center has improved collaboration among doctors, enhanced healthcare delivery to the public, and introduced new medical techniques to Zambian doctors through academic exchanges. ("Chinese medical team donates more telemedicine equipment to Zambian hospitals," 2017).

REFERENCES

杨洋. (2017, June 13). *Shanxi business builds Chinese-funded hospital in Zambia*. Global Edition. https://www.chinadaily.com.cn/m/shanxi/2017-06/13/content_29825357.htm

Administrator Ministry of Health. (2020, February 21). *China-Uganda friendship hospital Naguru*. Ministry of Health | Government of Uganda. https://www.health.go.ug/ sermon/china-uganda-friendship-hospital-naguru/

AfricaNews. (2018, August 31). *Chinese-donated hospital improves healthcare in Uganda*. Africanews. https://www.africanews.com/ 2018/08/31/ chinese-donated-hospital-improves-healthcare-in-uganda/

Alcorn, T. (2015). New orientation for China's health assistance to Africa. *Lancet*, *386*(10011), 2379–2380. doi:10.1016/S0140-6736(15)01232-5 PMID:26700520

Apolot, R. R., Ekirapa, E., Waldman, L., Morgan, R., Aanyu, C., Mutebi, A., Nyachwo, E. B., Seruwagi, G., & Kiwanuka, S. N. (2019). Maternal and newborn health needs for women with walking disabilities; "the twists and turns": A case study in Kibuku district Uganda. *International Journal for Equity in Health*, *18*(1), 43. Advance online publication. doi:10.118612939-019-0947-9 PMID:30866957

Blanford, J. I., Kumar, S., Luo, W., & MacEachren, A. M. (2012). It's a long, long walk: Accessibility to hospitals, maternity, and integrated health centers in Niger. *International Journal of Health Geographics, 11*(1), 24. doi:10.1186/1476-072X-11-24 PMID:22737990

Charge d'Affaires A.i. Zhu Qin meets with Zanny Minton Beddoes, editor of the economist. (2018, November 13). 欢迎访问中华人民共和国外交部网站. https://www.fmprc.gov.cn/ mfa_eng/ wjb_663304/ zwjg_665342/ zwbd_665378/ t1613081.shtml

Charles Chisala. (2017, June 7). *Hospital project takes Zambia, China ties to new high*. Zambia Daily Mail – Without fear or Favour. https://www.daily-mail.co.zm/ hospital-project-takes-zambia-china-ties-to-new-high/

China enters the global vaccine market. (2014). *Bulletin of the World Health Organization, 92*(9), 626-627. https://doi.org/ doi:10.2471/blt.14.020914

Chinese medical team donates more telemedicine equipment to Zambian hospitals. (2017, March 22). *The State Council of the People's Republic of China*. https://english.www.gov.cn/ news/international_exchanges/ 2017/03/22/ content_281475603372482.htm

Data: China-Africa trade — China Africa research initiative. (n.d.). *China Africa Research Initiative*. https://www.sais-cari.org/ data-china-africa-trade

Gavi, The Vaccine Alliance. (2017, June 29). *Gavi welcomes US$ 1.5 million contribution from China merchants group*. Gavi, the Vaccine Alliance. https:// www.gavi.org/ library/ news/ statements/ 2017/ gavi-welcomes-usd-1-5-million-contribution-from-china-merchants-group/

General Hospital of Niger / CADI. (2016, October 30). *ArchDaily*. https:// www.archdaily.com/798313/general-hospital-of-niger-cadi

in 5 children in Africa does not have access to life-saving vaccines. (2017). *WHO | Regional Office for Africa*. https://afro.who.int/ news/ 1-5-children-africa-do-not-have-access-life-saving-vaccines

Mei, H. (2018, April 26). *China's health aid to Africa takes diverse forms*. SSCP. https://www.csstoday.com/Item/5499.aspx

Moyimane, M. B., Matlala, S. F., & Kekana, M. P. (2017). Experiences of nurses on the critical shortage of medical equipment at a rural district hospital in South Africa: A qualitative study. *The Pan African Medical Journal*, *28*. Advance online publication. doi:10.11604/pamj.2017.28.100.11641 PMID:29515718

Murielle. (2016, August 17). *Niger inaugurates hospital constructed by China*. AFCHAM | The African Chamber of Commerce in China – Together We Build a Better Africa!! https://afcham-china.org/ niger-inaugurates-hospital-constructed-by-china/

Muula, A. S. (2005). Is there any solution to the "brain drain" of health professionals and knowledge from Africa? *Croatian Medical Journal*, *46*(1), 21–29. PMID:15726672

Ngosa, S. (2019, February 19). *Ministry of health » press release: Appointment of council members for the Levy Mwanawasa medical University (LMMU)*. Ministry of Health. https://www.moh.gov.zm/?p=6093

Olbrich, J., & Lili, G. (2018, November 7). *In China and for the World: Global Health Drug Discovery Institute (GHDDI) Embarks on a New Journey of Innovative Drug Discovery*. 清华大学新闻网. https://news.tsinghua.edu.cn/ publish/ thunewsen/ 9670/2018/ 20181115153933934515458/ 20181115153933934515458_.html

Ruinan, Z. (2018, August 20). *Africa welcomes Chinese investments in pharmaceutical industry*. Global Edition. https://www.chinadaily.com.cn/a/201808/20/WS5b7a7556a310add14f386bb1.html

Sen, A. K. (2018, September 18). *South Sudan: In South Sudan, it's deja Vu all over again*. allAfrica.com. https://allafrica.com/stories/201809180593.html

Shajalal, M., Xu, J., Jing, J., King, M., Zhang, J., Wang, P., Bouey, J., & Cheng, F. (2017). China's engagement with development assistance for health in Africa. *Global Health Research and Policy*, *2*(1), 24. Advance online publication. doi:10.118641256-017-0045-8 PMID:29202092

Skosana, I. (2015, October 7). *China to build 100 hospitals and clinics in Africa – Bhekisisa*. Bhekisisa. https://bhekisisa.org/ article/ 2015-10-07-china-to-build-100-hospitals-and-clinics-in-africa/

Smith, D. (2013, April 29). Chinese hospital heals sore spot in Zambia. *The Guardian*. https://www.theguardian.com/ global-development/ 2013/apr/29/ china-aid-build-hospital-zambia

Sow, M. (2018, September 6). Figures of the week: Chinese investment in Africa. *Brookings*. https://www.brookings.edu/ blog/africa-in-focus/ 2018/09/06/ figures-of-the-week-chinese-investment-in-africa/

Strydom, K., Ismail, F., & Frean, J. (2014). Plasmodium ovale: A case of not-so-benign tertian malaria. *Malaria Journal, 13*(1), 85. Advance online publication. doi:10.1186/1475-2875-13-85 PMID:24612535

Tadesse, K. (2017, October). *Enhancing healthcare-ChinAfrica*. https://www. chinafrica.cn/ Africa/201709/ t20170928_800105786.html

The World Bank. (n.d.). *Overview*. World Bank. https://www.worldbank.org/ en/country/niger/overview

Xinhua. (2017, October 27). *AU, China's ZTE launch smart health system project - Xinhua | English.news.cn*. 新华网_让新闻离你更近. https://www. xinhuanet.com// english/ 2017-10/27/ c_136708215.htm

Xinhua. (2018, May 15). *Zambia honors Chinese medical team for exemplary work - Xinhua | English.news.cn*. 新华网_让新闻离你更近. https://www. xinhuanet.com/ english/ 2018-05/15/ c_137178980_2.htm

Xinhua. (2018, May 19). *China donates medical equipment to assist Namibia's eye surgeries - Xinhua | English.news.cn*. 新华网_让新闻离你更近. https:// www.xinhuanet.com/ english/ 2018-05/19/ c_137189949.htm

Yayboke, E. (2018, November 27). *Accessing South Sudan: Humanitarian aid in a time of crisis*. Center for Strategic and International Studies. https:// www.csis.org/ analysis/ accessing-south-sudan-humanitarian-aid-time-crisis

Zheng, Y., Rodewald, L., Yang, J., Qin, Y., Pang, M., Feng, L., & Yu, H. (2018). The landscape of vaccines in China: History, classification, supply, and price. *BMC Infectious Diseases, 18*(1), 502. Advance online publication. doi:10.118612879-018-3422-0 PMID:30286735

Chapter 4
Healthcare Aid Between the USA and China During the Cold War

ABSTRACT

The best propaganda is not propaganda; instead, superpowers should provide resources to developing countries during this information age to enable economic growth. A country may obtain the outcomes it wants in the world politics because other countries—admiring its values, emulating its example, aspiring to its level of prosperity and openness—want to follow it. In this sense, it is also important to set the agenda and attract others in world politics and not only to force them to change by threatening military force or economic sanctions. This soft power—getting others to want the outcomes that you want—co-opts people rather than coercing them.

COLD WAR MEMO

On November 21, 1969, a memo from the United States Agency for International Development (USAID) Administrator of the Agency for International Development to President Nixon, Mr. John A. Hannah discussed the prospects for the AID (Agency for International Development) appropriation for Fiscal year 1970. He indicated that President Nixon had one advantage that you might be able to cash with Rep. Otto Passman (Chair House Appropriation Committee member) when the time was ripe and the stakes sufficiently high

DOI: 10.4018/978-1-7998-4450-1.ch004

for USAID. Since the 1970's there still has not been a critical time for USAID fiscal budget. Even though President Nixon and Mr. John A. Hannah agreed with the timing of an increase in budget for USAID. The time is now (the 1970's) today or tomorrow. These kind of discussions are still going on in the United States of American Congress today. The importance of USAID funds to meet the USA soft power goals and objectives has still not been met in the 21st century (CIA, 1980, P.166).

During the 1970s and 80s, the United States of America was a major contributor to the development of Africa's health care aid. This soft power strategy was the United States' approach in international development to win the heart and minds of Africans in the 1970s. According to Richard Nixon, (former U.S. president), "We intend to use our influence in international lending and development agencies to encourage greater assistance to Africa." (Nixon, 1973). The American people continued to assist through private and voluntary agencies and public programs, such as the World Health Organization, to help virtually eliminate the disease from Africa through humanitarian assistance (Nixon, 1973).

Africa's need for assistance can be measured by the fatal childhood diseases. "Adjustment programs are rending the fabric of African society. Of the estimated half a million child deaths in 1988 which can be related to the reversal or slowing down of development, approximately two-thirds were in Africa." (UNICEF, 1989). It has because of these statistics that the World Bank/International Monetary Fund, IMF, implemented the Structural Adjustment Program (PHC, 2) (Tambo, 2016).

Economic Impact

The Structural Adjustment Programs (SAP) was thought to represent economic growth and development was not known to have that reputation among Africa's poor majority. "African countries undergoing an SAP have been reported to have experienced rising rates of ill-health and mortality in both the urban and rural poor. (Loewenson, 1993). The lack of assistance to the ill children is due to the distance between the policymakers and the community. (Loewenson, 1993). The inability to improve the health of the citizens led to riots and unrest. "SAPs have been associated with increased food security and undernutrition, rising ill-health, and decreasing access to health care in two-thirds or more of the population of African countries that already live below poverty levels." (Loewenson, 1993). This policy created a split historical between these community and the policymakers. In Nigeria (1988)…a spontaneous uprising against the SAP, followed by a second demonstration in July 1989 (Loewenson, 1993). The cause of the increasing death tolls during this time was not solely due to the policies put in place but also lack of good governance.

In other parts of Africa rather than individual health, policies started to focus on the health of families and the community. The new agenda of the Pholela Health Centre in South Africa included, "mandatory immunizations; school-feeding schemes; the establishment of household and community food gardens; child growth monitoring, breastfeeding, and baby food supplementation; communal childcare services; and family planning." (Kautzky, et al. 2018). Organized by WHO and UNICEF the Alma Ata conference in 1978, adopted PHC as an international policy to model. "Pholela utilized population-based investigations to inform the provision of health services and incorporated health education and health promotion as essential elements of the health delivery system." (Kautzky, et al. 2018). Although a great contribution to "Healthcare for All" the policy ultimately failed to withstand time in Africa. "Further confusion was created in the decentralization of health services when many of the newly established districts of health boundaries failed to correspond administratively or geographically with redefined local government boundaries." (Kautzky, et al. 2018). Although, the initial policies set in place were backed by U.S. support they were not permanent solutions to deathly problems. China's approach to Africa's health development differs from that of the U.S. because the Chinese seems to have a hidden agenda.

Originally China's aid was insignificant and was used to promote the "One China" movement. China understood the shortcomings of the USAID and took the opportunity to strengthen its relations with Africa. "The Chinese government presented itself to African constituencies as a patron who rejected the imperial mandates of Western powers and understood the unique struggles of "peasant movements". (Youde, 2010). China's sudden interest is due to their new political plan, China's Africa Strategy. "Beijing's motives are clear. China's growing industries demand new energy and raw material suppliers; its exporters want markets; its diplomats require support in international organizations; and its propaganda still seeks support from allies to advance Chinese interests and, when necessary, to counter the United States." (Eisenman, & Kurlantzick, 2006). Even though this strategy is to grow the economy and international power, their change of direction also benefited Africa.

In the 70s one of the most successful aids in Africa was a Chinese medical team. (Youde, and Jeremy, 2010). "Historically, health diplomacy focused on international collaboration to protect human and commercial interests against the spread of particular infectious diseases." (Youde, et al., 2010). China provided medical teams alongside other economically based diplomats. Each province of China was responsible for whichever agreement to be implemented with the receiving state. "Under the terms of most of the medical cooperation agreements, the receiving state paid the expenses for the medical team. On occasion, the Chinese national government covered these costs through loans or grants." (Youde, et al., 2010). This strategy was one of the most beneficial programs implemented in Africa, although it was short-lived.

As the years went by China realized that the "African markets held little allure or promise for Chinese manufacturing interests" (Youde, et al., 2010). A Chinese commentator once said Africa, "counts for little in the overall scheme of Chinese foreign policy objectives." (Youde, et al., 2010). China exhibited soft power but did not exhibit a stable foundation. This lack of interest was regained decades later. "China's embracing of health diplomacy in Africa in recent years connects back to earlier efforts to promote itself as a vanguard alternative to leading Western states." (Youde, et al., 2010). The idea to empower Africa's healthcare, to build a strong international relationship is derived from the empowerment theory.

Theories to Support International Development

The empowerment theory, originally designed by Julian Rappaport in 1981, describes a theoretical model for understanding the process and consequences of efforts to exert control and influence over decisions that affect one's life, organizational functioning, and the quality of community life" (Rappaport, et al. 1984). Empowerment describes an ongoing process by which an individual learns to correspond to the relationship between their efforts and life outcomes. Health empowerment emphasizes facilitating one's awareness of the ability to participate knowingly in health and health care decisions (Shearer, 2009). A decision to make choices that have only positive effects on one's life represents the act of empowerment (Freire, 1973).

According to Woodroofe and Howard (2018), Vice President Mondale reported on the results of his just completed visit in 1978, to Nigeria, Senegal, Kenya, and Zimbabwe. He took to these countries a delegation of senior appointees in science and technology (e.g. heads of NASA, NSF, NIH, NOAA) and the Presidents of NAS, Ohio State and the University of Rochester. At each stop, we were received enthusiastically, and we achieved our goals of initiating or enhancing cooperation in major areas of development. In Nigeria and Senegal, we followed up on your recent visits. Africans were more into the western for support and innovation than the east.

He (Vice President Mondale) met even Prime Minister Mugabe who was at that time a darling of the western, Presidents Moi, Senghor and the Nigerian Vice President. All hold our country in the highest esteem. All are flattered and grateful for the President's sending the delegation, both for the political message it implies and the technological cooperation it portends (Woodroofe et al., 2018). At each of the four stops, he signed an agreement for cooperation in science and technology. These are to some extent symbolic but do provide a very useful framework for cooperation. He also signed specific agreements for carrying out major projects with the host countries. These are in areas of priority identified by those countries, typically agriculture and fisheries, energy, health, remote sensing, management, and manpower training. These projects will be funded by AID or the technical agencies, using money which is already programmed with the exception Nigeria which will pay for their assistance.

The health belief model was developed in the 1950s by the scientist and psychologist of the U.S. Public Health Service (Kruger, et al. 2016). These health Programs in sub – Sahara Africa were to increase diplomacy via soft power. Established meaningful health and technological support to further understand why people fail to embrace primary care for disease prevention in Africa. Primary care includes minor disease prevention strategies such as screening tests and vaccines. The health belief model suggests that a person's belief in the danger of any kind of illness along with that person's confidence in the adequacy of preventative measures will directly influence that person's engagement, or lack thereof, in those very measures.

Vice President Mondale believed more than ever that U.S. bilateral aid should emphasize technological assistance and PL 480 food; concessional aid should be shifted to the World Bank and other international lending agencies. This approach needs cost us no more than what we spend now (late 70's). At present, major opportunities are available to us for little additional funds. By reprogramming some $10 million (less than 10% of our assistance to these countries), we can develop a technical assistance program that would serve to solve many problems of Zimbabwe, Kenya and Senegal and bring us many political benefits (Woodroofe et al. 2018).

Maslow's hierarchy of needs theory in psychology, proposed by Abraham Maslow promotes the idea that human motivation drives a person's need to fulfill their basic needs (Mcleod, 2018). The fulfillment of these basic needs will help the motivations of all these sub-Sahara countries to build a more fruitful relationship with the United States. These very needs are illustrated through a pyramid of hierarchy broken down into five categories. At the top of the pyramid lies self-fulfillment needs, such as achieving one's full, creative potential. Other categories of needs support psychological needs, such as self-esteem. The bottom of the pyramid is a person's basic needs consisting of food, water, warmth, and rest.

It was first presented in 1943, where Maslow affirmed individuals must first please lower-level needs. However, these statements were later retracted when he explained how the attainment of needs is not an "all-or-none" anomaly and that the notion that "a need must be satisfied 100 percent before the next need emerges" is indeed false (Maslow, 1943). The United States should not have been in the position of "A need must be satisfied 100 percent before the next need emerges". We should be there and overlapping need to maintain soft power via economic developments and health care.

Carter (2005) was the first United States President Jimmy Carter to visit sub-Sahara Africa, Liberia and Nigeria in 1978. We (USA) chose, Nigeria because it was the largest and most influential African nation and Liberia because was founded by freed American slaves in the early 19th century. At that time, Liberia's President Tolbert was the leader of the Baptist World Alliance. This was the apex USA soft power diplomacy in Africa. Unfortunately, about a year later, Tolbert and 13 of his cabinet members were lined up and assassinated by insurrectionist Samuel Doe. President Carter was too busy with the Iranian hostage crisis and had to focus more on the Middle Eastern than Africa (NPR, 2015). This was a great missed opportunity to keep and maintain these relationships with Africans countries.

Central Intelligence Agency (CIA, 1980) describes the situation in West Africa that incumbent presidents have been in power since independence, and turnover at the top will affect the timing and manner of changes at other levels. Although there may be interim arrangements in some cases, it appears likely that West Africa will skip a generation when it makes its transition to new leadership. There would seem to be little future for the middle-aged group that has been overshadowed by the generation that led the way to independence. Within a few years, we expect to see younger people, now in their thirties and forties, whose ideas have been formed since independence move into positions of authority throughout the area [portion marking not declassified].

These young leaders are nominal members of the ruling party, as this is generally expected of officeholders, but few are active in party affairs and even fewer have indicated that they entertain presidential ambitions. Although in most West African societies it is considered bad form to discuss the possibility of change at the top, the reluctance of the young leaders to do so probably indicates a genuine lack of interest in political competition. When they do express views, they deplore the uncertainty and risk that comes with playing politics. In most instances, they aim to do well in their careers and to ensure a comfortable standard of living for themselves and their families [portion marking not declassified].

As these West African countries have matured, their elites have grown more similar. There has been an influx into key positions of young people from outlying areas where colonial influences are weaker and where tribal affiliations across national boundaries. Open borders and frequent multinational meetings strengthen regional ties—a trend recently reinforced by the return of Guinea to an active role in Africa [portion marking not declassified].

Coming administrations probably will be directed by highly educated Africans. They will have well-developed technical and managerial skills and yet be deeply rooted in African life. These potential leaders are professionally oriented people who show relatively little interest in ideology or political careers per se [portion marking not [decassified P. 166]. Under this second-generation leadership, the policy is likely to be increasingly shaped by a permanent civil service dedicated to solving the practical problems of nation-building, economic development, and regional cooperation. Although a strong presidential figure and a party apparatus will continue to mobilize the population in support of political goals, the dominance of party and president seems likely to diminish [declassified].

These countries are branching out from residual dependence on their former colonial rulers and turning more frequently to international organizations to meet development needs that are looming larger in their policy planning. They also are moving toward more formal inter-African cooperation with a variety of regional organizations that cross the old English- and French-speaking lines [portion marking not declassified].

Collectively these seven countries occupy the part of Sub-Saharan Africa that is geographically closest to the United States and Western Europe. They are generally pro-Western and have relatively open political systems. Although all of them are classified as less developed countries, their economies function relatively well, and several have considerable undeveloped resources. Although a severe economic setback could upset their stability, their political systems seem securely enough rooted to survive in normal conditions. Because they have been relatively friendly and trouble-free, these countries have only infrequently come to the attention of US policymakers. For that reason, the new generation coming to prominence is not well known in the United States, and there is some risk that this unfamiliarity could cause problems in future US dealings with them (CIA, 1980, PA-80-10171).

Here is a snapshot of the CIA memorandum in the 1980. Most of the analysis is true up until today, in the year 2021. Africans in some countries have lost three to four generations of leaders. The lack of a fair and balance broker to fill the void by the USA has been a strategic mistake. This void is still in the Africa continent, and it needs to be filled. Whoever would have filled this leadership void, could have been the most important partner with Africa. These partnership would have new African states than will yield significant diplomatic good will. Even though the United States had the best intelligence and situation analysis on the ground at the beginning of the 1980s. There was never a plan to win the heart and mind of the average African. The (USA) change of government and change of policy might have been one of the major reasons for this failure.

REFERENCES

CIA. (1980). *West Africa: The Second Generation*. https://history.state.gov/historicaldocuments/frus1977-80v17p2/d57

Eisenman, J., & Kurlantzick. (2006). China's Africa Strategy. *Current History (New York, N.Y.)*, 105.

Foreign Relations of the United States. 1977-1980, Volume XVII, Part 2, Sub-Saharan Africa. (2020). Paper Prepared in the National Foreign Assessment Center. https://history.state.gov/historicaldocuments/frus1969-76v04/d14

Freire, P. (1973). *Empowering education theory*. Harvard University Press.

Katuu, S. (2017). Healthcare systems: typologies, framework models, and South Africa's Health sector. *International Journal of Health Governance, 23*(2), 134-148. doi:10.1108/IJHG-10-2017-0054

Kautzky, K., & Tollman, S. M. (2018). A perspective on Primary Health Care in South Africa: Primary Health Care. Health Systems Trust (HST). *South African Health Review,* (1), 17 – 30. https://hdl.handle.net/10520/EJC35514

Kruger, J., Castor, T., & Kruger, D. (2016). Caffeine and Calorie Consumption at a College Campus Coffee Café. *Human Ethology Bulletin, 31*(1), 74–83. doi:10.22330/heb/311/074-083

Loewenson, R. (1993). Structural Adjustment and Health Policy in Africa. *International Journal of Health Services, 23*(4), 717–730. doi:10.2190/WBQL-B4JP-K1PP-J7Y3 PMID:8276531

Maslow, A. H. (1943). Conflict, frustration, and the theory of threat. *Journal of Abnormal and Social Psychology, 38*(1), 81–86. doi:10.1037/h0054634

Mcleod, S. (2018, May 21). *Maslow's Hierarchy of Needs*. Retrieved from March 20, 2020 from https://www.simplypsychology.org/maslow.html

Nixon, R. (1973). The United States Foreign Policy for the '70s: Shaping a Durable Peace (Africa). *Africa Today, 20*(2), 3–10. Retrieved March 13, 2020, from www.jstor.org/stable/4185296

Nye, J. (2004). *Soft Power: The Means to Success in World Politics*. Public Affairs.

Nye, J. (2012, May 8). China's Soft Power Deficit to catch up, its politics must unleash the many talents of its civil society. *The Wall Street Journal.*

Shearer, N. B. (2009). Health empowerment theory as a guide for practice. *Geriatric Nursing (New York, N.Y.), 30*(2, Suppl), 4–10. doi:10.1016/j.gerinurse.2009.02.003 PMID:19345857

Tambo, E., Ugwu, C. E., Guan, Y., & Wei, D. (2016). China-Africa Health Development Initiatives: Benefits and Implications for Shaping Innovative and Evidence-informed National Health Policies and Programs in Sub-Saharan African Countries. (United States). *International Journal Maternal Childs AIDS., 5*(2), 119–133. doi:10.21106/ijma.100 PMID:28058199

The Carter Center. (2005, October 8). *Jimmy Carter's Trip Report: Liberia and Ghana.* https://www.cartercenter.org/news/documents/doc2221.html

Woodroofe, P. L., & Howard, A. M. (2018). *Foreign Relations of the United States, 1977-1980, Volume XVII, Part 2, Sub-Saharan Africa United States.* Government Publishing Office. https://history.state.gov/historicaldocuments/frus1977-80v17p23

Youde, J. (2010). China's Health Diplomacy in Africa. China. *International Journal (Toronto, Ont.)*, *8*(1), 151–163. Advance online publication. doi:10.1142/S0219747210000099

Chapter 5
The History and Overall Economic Influence of Chinese Healthcare Aid in Africa

ABSTRACT

The motivation of the Chinese on soft power economic development goes beyond healthcare diplomacy. Chinese firms and construction projects are all over the African continent. Across the continent, there has also been a noticeable decline in American hospitals being built in relation to Chinese hospitals being built. This has been one of the factors contributing to the reduction of the USA's previous hold on economic development throughout Africa. Notably, China has increased its involvement in global health governance. As the largest developing country and the second largest economy in the world, China's engagement in global health governance should be given considerable attention as the PRC has been providing medical assistance in various ways to African now for almost six decades. Despite initial concerns, this has steadily continued even throughout COVID-19.

INTRODUCTION: MOTIVATION FOR INVOLVEMENT

In recent years, China has increased its involvement in global health governance. As the largest developing country and the second largest economy in the world, China's engagement in global health governance should be given considerable attention (Wang & Sun, 2014). It is, however, important to note

DOI: 10.4018/978-1-7998-4450-1.ch005

that the country has been providing medical assistance in various ways to Africa for nearly six decades. The criticism of this aid, nevertheless, lies in the lack of understanding of China's motivation. China is a developing country, so its continuous charitable gestures in sending its own medical resources to several nations within the African continent seems quite unconventional.

Initially, Chinese officials have offered an explanation stating that their motivation for doing such is primarily for a humanitarian purpose (Wang & Sun, 2014). Yet, we cannot completely disregard the potential political considerations. Researchers assert that other explanations for medical assistance to Africa may have been driven by its conflict with Taiwan for a seat in the United Nations. Other possible reasons could be to create opportunities to extend its socialist ideologies overseas, or to better its own international appearance as an approach to address the challenges it faces within an evolving international context (Wang & Sun, 2014).

Then again, China's health diplomacy could be meant to offer something more altruistic. The country emphasizes the importance of health financing when declaring its health development commitment. Although it does make major investments in Africa, these are to maximize gains and opportunities by creating efficient systems that value health as a priority (Tambo, et al., 2016). This effort to create healthcare relationships does also play a role in supporting the country's efforts for research projects, resource sharing, and in promoting mutualistic trade, growth, and stability (Tambo, et al., 2016). The amount of healthcare support China has given to African countries, can be represented by their continuous investment of nearly 80 million USD each year since 2007 (Wang & Sun, 2014). This roughly translates to 1.8 million USD to each country it supports (Wang & Sun, 2014). This, however, only makes up a small portion of its support budget for international aid, which totals 256.29 billion Chinese yuan. Of this amount, 6% of its healthcare aid is used towards free grants and 3% is used for loans in public facilities of Africa (Wang & Sun, 2014). Another source claims that by 2009, nearly 45.7 of china's total aid was given to Africa. These contradicting numbers reveal another issue with the design and the motivations of the Chinese government.

China not only limits itself in global health dialogues but refuses to allow careful evaluation of its health assistance investments (Lin, et al., 2016). As a result, this makes it very difficult to accurately keep track of the actual amount of aid it gives. The government also heavily encourages Chinese firms to think in the medium term.

Africa demands the most pharmaceuticals which can and does allow Chinese pharmaceutical companies to intervene and promote Chinese alternative medicine. This opens doors for future business partnerships where Chinese companies can offer active ingredients at favorable credit terms and the best local prices. This is only possible due to the relative inexpensiveness of Chinese alternative medicine in relation to western medicine. This creates a major challenge for allopathic medicine on its own to persist as the primary and/or sole form treatment within many African nations (Alcorn, 2015). In fact, if pharmaceutical companies were to establish business within Africa, research indicates that there would be a major decrease in the cost of production of its pharmaceuticals, allowing them to sell their products at a competitive price (Alcorn, 2015).

The conceptualization and implementation of China's medical assistance is described to be a "no strings attached system." The country declares that never impose on ideology, values, and the development models of other countries, as African nations should be able to rule themselves (Lin, et al., 2016). This, along with the recent announcement of 60 billion USD by President Xi Jinping to support public health in Africa after the second summit of the Forum on China-Africa Cooperation, it becomes difficult to question if country has any precise self-centered motivations (Lin, et al., 2016). China's efforts in aiding Africa seem to be widespread within the nation. Provincial governments are designated to provide medical teams to different areas of Africa. The only issue with this is the allocation of resources varies by different provincial health projects. However, this does not necessarily undermine the persistent effort that is being made. China does, nevertheless, maintain a certain level of expectations from its beneficiaries. Although there are no major or credible indications of the country's intent of exploiting African supplies of oil and natural resources, it does import a significant amount of minerals, raw materials, and oil from countries such as Sudan and Angola. It does, nonetheless, expect certain loyalties. This can be seen from the withdrawal of its medical teams from recipient countries that established diplomatic relationships with Taiwan, supported Tibet, and that supported the status of the Uyghur people during the 1980s and 1990s (Wang & Sun, 2014). In other words, we can make the implication that China does and will not support African nations that bite the hand that feeds them.

China's relationship with Africa has served as a counterbalance to the powers of the United States and Russia. Unfortunately, with its minimal involvement in intercontinental African governments, it has indirectly supported the outcome and prevalence of many monarchies, authoritarian regimes, and pseudo-republics (oligarchies). Despite its aid, China does still prioritize itself. Towards the end of the latter half of the 20th century, it decreased its medical assistance in an attempt to focus and establish its place in the international market. With all of this in mind, it is fair to say assume that china is not entirely "altruistic." On the other hand, it is also unjust to assert that it is entirely "opportunistic" as it does involve itself heavily in international aid. Rather, the best means of analyzing China's ideology and motivation is to incorporate a dual understanding of both its developmental needs as a country and its government's ambition in establishing and presenting itself as a demonstrative world power. Simply, put, China is strategic. It promotes itself by promoting and helping others without expecting any major return beyond international friendship and mutualistic support. Whether this is a good or bad thing is an individual matter of perspective, but it, nonetheless, does give reason to investigate the history and impact of the Chinese "pro-bono" healthcare aid in Africa.

Historical Involvement

Modern Chinese diplomatic involvement in Africa goes back to the 1950s. During these interactions, China sought to frame its relationships with African governments through anti-colonialism and counterweighting the presence of the United States and Soviet Union. China took advantage of its developing and presented itself to be like Africa. It rejected imperial mandates of western powers, and understood the nature and struggles found within peasant movements. Throughout the 1950s and 1960s, China promoted Maoism and anti-colonialism as a model for development, but also provided support for revolutionary movements throughout the continent without imposing its ideologies. Initially, China only focused its efforts in rural healthcare development and sent teams comprised of healthcare professionals from multiple specialties. However, China, strategically, also ensured that many of their health aid projects also coincided with their other diplomatic infrastructure projects in Africa, such as the TanZam Railway project in the 1970s (Youde, 2010).

This allowed China's influence to grow significantly, as it was able to show its commitment in bettering the countries of Africa overall. It is interesting to note, however, that during most of the latter half of the 20th century, funding for healthcare aid projects came directly from the national health care budget. The period between1971-1978 has been regarded as a period of rapid increase in China's foreign aid. In fact, during the 1960s and 1970s, China had provided not only the best form of healthcare aid in Africa, but also did so while providing quality medical care in resource-poor settings. This was primarily because China emphasized the need for preventative care instead of emergency care, which in many cases is much more expensive to provide (Youde, 2010). China's main goal at this time was to create partnerships and friendships instead of robbing the continent of its natural resources. Eventually this evolved into a more mutualistic relation. China did this with an "I scratch your back, and you can scratch mine" approach.

By 1993, China became a major net importer of oil from Africa. It is projected to rely on imports for 45 percent of its total consumption, as the average production cost of onshore oil is relatively expensive (Taylor, 2015). As a result, China was able to continue its rate of economic growth through the ways of securing stable import supplies of oil and natural resources (Youde, 2010). This is due to the linkages made with Angola, Nigeria, and Sudan. This shows how its non-conditionality aid was not only appealing but influenced signs of trust among war-torn regions. By the 1980s and 1990s, however, China did begin withdrawing several of its medical teams. After a breach in diplomatic links in 1979, the Chinese medical cooperation discontinued in many countries such as Cameroon, Ethiopia, and Chad. Albeit the reasons usually varied per country, they mostly encompassed the risk of losing physicians in countries facing internal strife and war. However, in replacement of healthcare, China did provide weapons. Reports indicate that nearly 10 percent of total conventional arms came from China between 1996 and 2003 (Taylor, 2015). In this manner, China never actually withdrew involvement or interest in African countries.

China reinvigorated its efforts in bettering Africa during the premise of the 21st century. Now, achieving a status as an international power, it found the need to maintain its status. In October 2000, at the inaugural of the China Africa Cooperation Forum, China forgave 1.2 billion dollars of USD of foreign debt and pledged to increase its diminishing aid contributions to improve several aspects of Africa, particularly health. Health seems to be the main priority of the "New Chinese effort." This is seen in the 2006 CACF meeting, where China pledged to donate 5 billion dollars in loans to the entire continent while also stating its intent in building more hospitals and creating health and education programs throughout the continent (Youde, 2010). This was an essential move for China to make, as it not only portrayed that its continued interest in international assistance, but also its willingness to both improve healthcare facilities and train doctors in Africa. Moreover, they also emphasized their intent to create treatments that would prevent and cure major widespread diseases, such as Malaria and HIV/AIDS.

In 2005, 900 Chinese medical personnel had been serving in nearly 35 states. In 2007, China had approximately 4,000 general practitioners with the government estimating a need of at least 160,000 to meet the country's medical needs (Youde, 2010). This made the Chinese international health aid movement seem even more prominent and generous. The lack of medical professionals at home, however, implied that if further shortage were to occur, then the Chinese government would need to send pharmaceutical and medical technology as replacement. This would be considered a valiant effort but would not be as impactful in terms of aid than having an actual Chinese presence. Chinese firms did, however, begin investing and establishing companies within the African continent. Unfortunately, this does not come without loss, as the impact in Nigeria alone cost a loss of an estimated 2 million jobs due to Chinese competition (Youde, 2010).

Between 2006 to 2015, it is estimated that China's development assistance for health distributed projects within 670 subdivisions of 50 African countries (Yang, Liu, & Guo, 2018). Many of the projects were allocated within the western and eastern coasts of Africa, although Chinese medical teams were also dispatched to northern Africa (Yang, Liu, & Guo, 2018). As a result of its health aid, African support within the UN for China has become commonplace. This is seen especially when China's human rights records have been put under the spotlight. Likewise, China also "supports" Africa in many of its issues. This can be seen by China's continuous support in refusing to intervene and impose sanctions within the UN towards African countries by not voting for sanctions against Sudan. It instead declared its support to find a political solution to the crisis and offer humanitarian support (Shichor, 2005).

Targeting Specific Diseases

China has made much progress in many domains of global health (Liu, 2014). It deploys medical teams, constructs facilities, donates drugs and equipment, and trains personnel (Liu, 2014). Above all, it also has made great efforts in controlling and targeting specific diseases in Africa as it has been prompted by its own challenges with disease. In 2009, China's Ministry of Health stated that the 2003 Severe acute respiratory syndrome (SARS) outbreak had alerted both the citizens and the government about the dangers of infectious disease not only to their country but to nations worldwide (Chan, et al, 2010). After this, China accepted the international influence of the World Health Organization and made major reforms. Due to the SARS epidemic, China faced a 6.1-billion-dollar loss, which, although paltry in comparison to its national GDP, was enough to see the need for improvement in its public health care system (Chan, et al, 2010). As a result, this led to an overall increase of 100% spending in domestic health between 2002 and 2005. By 2007, public health accounted for 0.89% of the country's GDP. In 2010, the government also made the decision to provide its rural resident with more equitable and accessible health care and improve its overall surveillance of diseases (Chan, et al. 2010). Another disease that has remained a public health issue is schistosomiasis. China was once highly endemic to the disease but has made substantial progress and is now moving to eliminate the disease across sub-Saharan Africa. Thus, in effect, China builds off its own experiences to promote global health. While doing this, it also strikes a balance between national sovereignty and collective responsibility by using a "mix of hard and soft" instruments of national power to induce change in recipient countries.

Tropical diseases and epidemics are a major threat to the health and normal life of Africans. One of China's biggest priorities in Africa has been to eradicate and prevent the spread of malaria. Many countries have faced challenges in controlling malaria due to the outreach limitations in public health system and their poor primary health care infrastructure (Xia, et al. 2014). Malaria is the number one killer and about one million children die of it annually in Africa (Anshan, 2011). As a result, China has been making efforts to strategically implement controlling measures through the National Malaria Control Program (Xia, et al. 2014). They have sent Chinese medical teams to distribute free medications, specifically Cotecxin, which has reputably been an effective anti-malaria drug in Africa (Anshan, 2011). Within the last half century, China has constructed over thirty hospital and malaria treatment centers throughout the continent of Africa as a response to disease (Saibou, 2017). This has allowed many to not only receive quality treatment but also eliminates and reduces the need to travel long distances and having to pay expensive prices at private hospitals (Saibou, 2017).

China also played an active role in the global fight against the 2014 outbreak of the Ebola virus disease. It provided support in West Africa and supplied medical experts, scientists and supplies to the affected countries (Lu, (2015). In fact, China was the largest contributor, providing 120 million dollars of financial, technical, material and human resources to the most affected countries (Saibou, 2017). It even set up treatment and research centers in Sierra Leone for Tropical diseases. It is important to acknowledge that the virus also posed a threat to China, as well. Due to its ability to rapidly spread, Ebola became a priority for the Chinese government to eliminate in order to maintain the stability of its own public health system and continue the growth of its economy. China did this through multi-sector control efforts, where medical teams trained people from local communities to teach and encourage local residents the different ways of combating the disease (Lu, 2015). Although there were challenges, specifically in areas that lacked sanitary conditions and healthcare facilities, China was still able to prevail through the influence of its consistent aid and medical expertise.

China has also contributed something very important to Africa. During epidemic outbreaks, it has not only improved the public health systems in Africa, but more importantly has raised the standards of local medical services within African countries. This, however, does not solve the continents critical shortage of medical personnel, which as mentioned previously is an issue that China faces itself. As Africa comprises 60% percent of the world's population of HIV/AIDs patients and the highest incidence and mortality for Cholera, there are still many issues that China can assist in. In fact, one neglected issue has been the lack of medical attention put in treating Hepatitis B Virus. Although there is a vaccine for the disease, large working populations can be diminished from the silent pandemic (Saibou, 2017). Many can also not obtain treatments as treatments for the disease are expensive. As a result, the disease is expected to make a disaster appearance if not controlled properly within the coming years (Saibou, 2017). Yet, leaders of both China and West Africa have not given much attention to its prevention in comparison to other diseases.

Overall Impact and Potential Benefits of Chinese Healthcare and Medicine

For some China represents a hope for opportunity and progress, while for others it is seen as a threat (Naidu & Mbazima, 2008). The Chinese believe that serving people is the fundamental aim of public health systems. Patient trust is a critical determinant of health seeking behaviors and health outcomes (Mclaughlin, 27). As a result, Chinese physicians make great efforts in building patient trust not just abroad, but also at home. In a study completed at a health facility in Guangzhou, African Migrants expressed great levels of trust with Chinese physicians despite language barriers and general mistrust of Chinese healthcare providers in general. This was all influenced by factors such as interpersonal communication, respective social network, the individual perspective of the health system, and the respective individual socio-cultural levels. Many claimed that their slight mistrust was by the fact that payment collection was completed at the time of registration versus after their visit, a practice different from their homelands. This expressed an emphasis of money to the migrant patients (Mclaughlin, 27). In another study also conducted in Guangzhou, we see similar results where African migrants expressed a high level of satisfaction with their physicians but did find issues with language problems (Mathews, 25). This emphasis on care and trust domestically is well translated in its approach to global health.

China's global engagement is likely to grow and reshape the atmosphere of global health (Fink, 2002). While seen in its involvement in Africa, an integral part of its healthcare is the incorporation of alternative medicine. In some African countries, the use of traditional medicine for basic healthcare needs ranges up to 90% (Fink, 2002). The integration of Chinese medicine with allopathic treatments in China's healthcare essentially enhances the trust in its effect. In many African populations, there is a trust in traditional medicine for basic health care needs due to the time and evaluative commitment and personability of traditional healers. China's emphasis on these forms of treatment allow African patients a level of comfort due to familiarity. Still, many Africans fear that medical professionals do not respect traditional healers and will lower the quality of their care if they knew, and thus do not report the use of traditional medicine (Fink, 2002). Whether traditional Chinese medicine works by itself is a topic up for discussion, however, simply undermining the positive benefits of certain medical practices as placebo despite their reported use for centuries leads to a risk of overlooking treatments that, if used in conjunction with western medicine, may bring about major benefits. Currently, the challenge with Chinese healthcare is the lack of coordination between traditional healers and official health care systems and practitioners (Fink, 2002). This poses major risks for patients. For example, the use of ginseng and warfarin in combination can cause a potentially harmful interaction resulting in blood thinning.

The combination of herbal medicine and allopathic medicine is vaguely understood however China is benefiting in trust by Africans by combining allopathic treatment with traditional treatment within their foreign aid facilities. In fact, the gap between traditional and allopathic medicine is even less understood in Africa, as many traditional healers were ban from practice during colonial times (Fink, 2002). Unusually, however, the use of alternative medicine is different in both developed and in developing countries. While the majority within developing countries use it as a necessity for basic medical care, individuals in developing countries use it for problems related to aging and chronic diseases. Fortunately, the combination of use has seen progress. The Joint United Nations Program on HIV/AIDS recently reviewed collaboration with traditional medicine practitioners in AIDS prevention and care in 9 African countries. However, there is a serious lack of willingness among donors to fund research of such practices (Fink, 2002). Certain Chinese herbal remedies, such as Artemisia annual, have been found effective at treating resistant malaria. In fact, nearly a fourth of modern medicine, is derived from traditional plant medicine and procedures such as acupuncture have been proven to show signs of relaxation and alleviation of both mood and sleeping disorders (Fink, 2002). Thus, it is important that both traditional healers and physicians consider and get the word out of each other's respective medicines. Chinese healthcare is dismissing neither and using its innovation to produce treatments even within research facilities within Africa.

Suggestions for US Foreign Aid

It is difficult to ignore the overall impact that China's Healthcare aid has on an economic level. It would, however, be beneficial to compare the aid of China with that of US towards Africa to gain a better sense of how much China's initial Healthcare effort have allowed it to expand in its terms of Chinese-African mutual partnerships. It is interesting to note that China's aid shows a positive effect on its total volume of trade and imports from Africa, while aid from the US has exhibited little impact (Liu & Tang, 2018). One reason may be the difference in national interests of support. Generally, an aide-trade relationship should promote bilateral trade flow between the donor and recipient. After the founding of the Official Development Assistance program, African countries have received a large share of the total disbursements, yet still are unable to upgrade their economic performance. The US is the largest donor to Africa however it ties its donations with conditionality and selectivity. This is opposite to China which offers unconditional aid through South-South cooperation. This has allowed it to structure mutual benefits with African countries. This form of support, however, is criticized in that it enables non-democratic regimes to persist and may be a sign of countering the Western hemisphere's attempt of promoting democratic governance. Furthermore, African nations also tend to import significantly more products from China than the US (Liu & Tang, 2018). Although this may be due to differences in price manufacturing and sale, it enables China to sell and export its products to Africa at lower costs. Another reason this could be is simply because China does not force its beneficiaries to participate in trade, but simply requests to form partnerships with them.

Both China and America's foreign aid programs have similarities. They both are complexly operated by different agencies: China is operated by the Ministry of Commerce and the Export-import Bank, while the United States is operated by the Department of Defense and the US Agency for International Defense. Both countries also only provide aid to states with whom they have diplomatic ties with, unless it is to support a nation during a natural disaster. However, the United States emphasizes and allocates most of its aid in Health support, while China provides aid primarily for infrastructure (Boynton, 2011). Due to the ongoing struggle of fighting infectious diseases in Africa, perhaps China's aid in infrastructure is valued more since its effects are visibly longer lasting. In addition, China also prioritizes the requests of local leaders while the United States consults the host government (Boynton, 2011). In many African states where government is often decentralized or unfavored by their people, China gains an upper advantage by creating projects and focusing on the needs of local people.

It would ultimately be in the US's best interest to work with China in providing foreign aid to the continent of Africa (Brown, Liang, Hale, & Novotny, 2013). This could allow the US to gain similar benefits as China in terms of economic partnership. One way of doing so would be to

loosen their conditionality statements when giving aid. In terms of health aid, the US should take the time of understanding the local regions they are supporting and modifying their delivery of medicine with an integration of African traditional medicine. This will not only enhance the credibility of the US but will also enhance its likeability for incorporating common practice from target regions, allowing comfortability. In addition, it may introduce new pharmaceutical and medical research pursuits that could result in new and more effective forms of treatment towards infectious diseases.

If the US were to collaborate with China in their aid towards Africa, it could allow for a step in easing the tense and polarized relationship already existing between the two nations. Collaborative efforts have already been seen towards global health diplomacy, such as in combating the Ebola virus disease and in the fight against AIDs/HIV. Perhaps, healthcare aid could be the starting point for partnership. However, in order to do such, both countries would need to compromise and be willing to learn about each other's approach to healthcare delivery. Using this as a basis, the US could also propose working with China in its efforts to promote infrastructure. It would be unlikely for China to dismiss this support, as it could indicate a self-seeking intent to maintain its influence so that it may be the primary beneficiary of the continents oil, natural resources, and be one of its highest product exporters. Although this would require many adjustments to the US's diplomacy, it could potentially balance China's majority influence within the continent, allowing the US to further strengthen its ties and favorability with more nations.

Lastly, it is important to note that in 2008, the US-Africa trade was estimated to be 100 billion USD (Dinko, 2021). In 2019, this number had reportedly decreased to 56 billion USD (Dinko, 2021). In contrast, China's trade increased from 102 billion USD to 192 billion USD during this time period (Dinko, 2021). This surge has made China the largest growing investor in Africa at this time (Dinko, 2021). Being a world leader, the USA has specifically faced severe criticism across the globe for not helping developing countries early during the COVID-19 global health emergency (Gauttam, Kaur, & Singh, 2020). This, as a result, leaves a much desirable recommitment to Africa in order to catch up to the momentum of China.

COVID-19 and Future Predictions for Chinese Health Aid in Africa

There are many concerns with the future of China's foreign health aid efforts. China's selectivity of focusing on certain diseases such malaria and HIV/AIDs while ignoring others such as cholera and hepatitis B, shows that there is a need of increasing their health donations and expanding their research and treatment efforts. Otherwise, many populations may find themselves suffering from outbreaks of controllable diseases. Another concern lies in the future of alternative medicine. Unless China makes more valiant attempts of researching, promoting, and integrating its traditional medicine with allopathic medicine, it will continue to be considered a nonconventional form of practice. In recent years, there has also been a growing number of quack doctors who have emerged and established third-rate private clinics in Africa. These individuals are representative of scam businesses that ship faulty medical devices and placebo medicine to sell to locals who have put their trust in Chinese healthcare. Both the Chinese and respective states of Africa need to identify these charlatans, as they endanger the lives of many innocent people seeking treatment and are damaging the credibility and reputation of Chinese health diplomacy. In addition, the structure and standard of the Chinese Medical Team program has remained mostly unchanged. The organization and its management are much to be desired as it has undergone little internal or external evaluation in the last 50 years. For this reason, it is difficult to hold the team accountable and up to standard. This becomes crucial as China has continued to expand its south-south cooperation in economics, trade, and health. Thus, improving the CMTs, which had been the key players in initially gaining trust from African nations, is essential in improving health in Africa and in establishing the continents self-sustainability. This, indirectly, will strengthen China's role and engagement in international diplomacy and in domestic progression.

The United Nations Economic Commission for Africa estimates that Africa's financial gap is $66 billion per year, while also taking on 24 percent of the world's health burden with approximately 16 percent of the global population. Yet, it still only receives 1 percent of global health spending, indicating a need for more infrastructural investment, job creation, and increase production and exportation. Although China is making a valiant effort in developing the infrastructure of many African countries, it must also prioritize many of the most basic necessities of the land. Food quality, production, preservation can be compromised due to the extreme climate and famine may ensue in many areas. Furthermore, creating sustainable water pipelines and treatment storage sites are also necessary to ensure the wellbeing of the people of Africa. If these areas are all targeted through expanded investment and foreign aid donations, both Africa and China will mutually benefit in not only health but also in economy.

With the emergence of COVID-19, China has used the pandemic to promote its "Health Silk Road" diplomacy to reaffirm its geopolitical and geostrategic influences (Gauttam, Kaur, & Singh, 2020). This has been a constructive response that has helped the nation dismiss many of the criticisms it has received in its initial idleness in preventing the spread of COVID-19.

This is also creating a potential set-up for China to emerge as the leading Superpower during this emergency, as it has communicated that it would like to help aid Africa, despite major suspicions of its intentions (Asiedu, 2020).

As many African states entered recessions for the first time in several decades, debt relief became a necessity to prevent long-term economic collapses (Bone & Cinotto, 2020). As the largest nation to credit the Continent, China endorsed the G-20 Debt Service Suspension Initiative for the poorest countries in the world and suspended principal repayments and interest payments from May 1st of 2020 to the end of 2020 (Sun, 2020). Moreover, China also pledged at the 73rd World Health Assembly that it would provide 2 billion USD to help with the COVID-19 response and in supporting developing countries through economic and social development over the span of two years as a form of international assistance (Sun, 2020).

China sent its first pandemic assistance to African states in late March of 2020 (Chaziza, 2021). Assistance was specifically donations provided by the Chinese government, Chinese state-owned enterprises (SOEs), and Chinese private firms through the facilitation of Chinese embassies in African states (Chaziza, 2021). The first donations distributed Personal Protective Equipment (PPE) and other medical supplies as a way to promote China's "Mask Diplomacy" in Africa.

China began by sending medical experts and supplies to Maghreb countries to control the spread of the pandemic (Chaziza, 2021). For example, Algeria, a close ally and its largest trade partner, not only received medical supplies but also was assisted in laying out plans to establish a small hospital for preventative care (Chaziza, 2021).

However, it is during the second wave of the pandemic that China made its statement as a global leader by joining the Covax Alliance and promising assistance through the production and distribution of COVID-19 vaccine (Bone, & Cinotto, 2020). While its vaccine rollout has been moving much slower than anticipated, China pledges to distribute 2 billion doses of a COVID-19 vaccine by the end of 2021, particularly delivering free vaccines to Africa (Bone, & Cinotto, 2020). Thus, as China began this pandemic with an anticipated downturn in its relations with Africa, it has since been attempting to make restitution for the negative impact COVID-19 has had on its African allies. While the long-term impact COVID-19 will have on Chinese-African relations is still unclear, what is clear that Chinese health aid will continue at least throughout this global emergency.

REFERENCES

Alcorn, T. (2015, December 12). New orientation for China's health assistance to Africa. *The Lancet*. https://www.thelancet.com/journals/lancet/article/PIIS0140-6736(15)01232-5/fulltext

Asiedu, K. G. (2020, April 8). *China wants to help Africa fight coronavirus but not everyone is welcoming*. QuartzAfrica. https://qz.com/africa/1834670/chinese-medical-aid-for-covid-19-in-africa-gets-mixed-support/

Bone, R. M., & Cinotto, F. (2020, November 2). *China's Multifaceted COVID-19 Diplomacy Across Africa*. The Diplomat. https://thediplomat.com/2020/11/chinas-multifaceted-covid-19-diplomacy-across-africa/

Boynton, X. L. (2017, July 25). *China's Emerging Global Health and Foreign Aid Engagement*. China's Emerging Global Health and Foreign Aid Engagement | Center for Strategic and International Studies. https://www.csis.org/blogs/smart-global-health/chinas-emerging-global-health-and-foreign-aid-engagement

Brown, M., Liang, B. A., Hale, B., & Novotny, T. (2013). *China's Role in Global Health Diplomacy: Designing Expanded U.S. Partnership for Health System Strengthening in Africa*. Global Health Governance. http://blogs.shu.edu/ghg/2013/09/17/chinas-role-in-global-health-diplomacy-designing-expanded-u-s-partnership-for-health-system-strengthening-in-africa-2/

Chan, L.-H., Chen, L., & Xu, J. (2010, April 27). *China's Engagement with Global Health Diplomacy: Was SARS a Watershed?* PLOS Medicine. https://journals.plos.org/plosmedicine/article?id=10.1371%2Fjournal.pmed.1000266

Chaziza, M. (2021, February 17). *Chinese Health Diplomacy and the Maghreb in the COVID-19 Era*. Middle East Institute. https://mei.edu/publications/chinese-health-diplomacy-and-maghreb-covid-19-era

Chen, S., Pender, M., Jin, N., Merson, M., Tang, S., & Gloyd, S. (2019, February 28). Chinese medical teams in Africa: a flagship program facing formidable challenges. *Journal of Global Health*. https://pubmed.ncbi.nlm.nih.gov/30842880/

Dinko, D. H. (2021, March 10). *China's 'mask diplomacy' wins influence across Africa, during and after the pandemic*. The Conversation. https://theconversation.com/chinas-mask-diplomacy-wins-influence-across-africa-during-and-after-the-pandemic-153048

Fan, H.-J., Gao, H.-W., Ding, H., Zhang, B.-K., & Hou, S.-K. (2015, January 7). *The Ebola Threat: China's Response to the West African Epidemic and National Development of Prevention and Control Policies and Infrastructure: Disaster Medicine and Public Health Preparedness*. Cambridge Core. https://www.cambridge.org/core/journals/disaster-medicine-and-public-health-preparedness/article/ebola-threat-chinas-response-to-the-west-african-epidemic-and-national-development-of-prevention-and-control-policies-and-infrastructure/878680DED3335407DDFAC62333434F88

Fink, S. (2002, November). International efforts spotlight traditional, complementary, and alternative medicine. *American Journal of Public Health*. https://www.ncbi.nlm.nih.gov/pmc/articles/PMC3221476/

Gauttam, P., Singh, B., & Kaur, J. (2020, October 12). *COVID-19 and Chinese Global Health Diplomacy: Geopolitical Opportunity for China's Hegemony?* SAGE Journals. https://journals.sagepub.com/doi/full/10.1177/0976399620959771

Grepin, K. A., Fan, V. Y., Shen, G. C., & Chen, L. (1970, January 1). *China's role as a global health donor in Africa: what can we learn from studying under reported resource flows?* Globalization and Health. https://globalizationandhealth.biomedcentral.com/articles/10.1186/s12992-014-0084-6

Li, A. (2011, January). *Chinese medical cooperation in Africa: with special emphasis on the medical teams and anti-malaria campaign*. Eldis. https://www.eldis.org/document/A63343

Lin, S., Gao, L., Reyes, M., Cheng, F., Kaufman, J., & El-Sadr, W. M. (1970, January 1). *China's health assistance to Africa: opportunism or altruism?* Globalization and Health. https://globalizationandhealth.biomedcentral.com/articles/10.1186/s12992-016-0217-1

Liu, A., & Tang, B. (2018, April). US and China aid to Africa: Impact on the donor-recipient trade relations. *China Economic Review*. https://www.sciencedirect.com/science/article/pii/S1043951X17301566

Liu, P., Guo, Y., Qian, X., Tang, S., Li, Z., & Chen, L. (2014, August 30). China's distinctive engagement in global health. *The Lancet*. https://www.thelancet.com/journals/lancet/article/PIIS0140-6736(14)60725-X/fulltext

Lu, H. (2015, November). *China takes an active role in combating an Ebola outbreak: On-site observations and reflections from a Chinese healthcare provider*. Intractable & rare diseases research. https://www.ncbi.nlm.nih.gov/pmc/articles/PMC4660866/

Mathews, G. (2015, December 1). *Africans in Guangzhou - Gordon Mathews, 2015*. SAGE Journals. https://journals.sagepub.com/doi/full/10.1177/186810261504400402

McLaughlin, M. M., Simonson, L., Zou, X., Ling, L., & Tucker, J. D. (2015, May 12). *African migrant patients' trust in Chinese physicians: a social ecological approach to understanding patient-physician trust*. PloS one. https://pubmed.ncbi.nlm.nih.gov/25965064/

Morangi, L. (2019, February 14). *Africa urges investment in healthcare*. ChinaDaily. http://www.chinadaily.com.cn/a/201902/14/WS5c64d097a3106c65c34e94ba.html

Naidu, S., & Mbazima, D. (2008, February 29). *China–African relations: A new impulse in a changing continental landscape*. Futures. https://www.sciencedirect.com/science/article/pii/S001632870800030X

Saibou, F. (2017, May 9). *Impact of China-West Africa healthcare cooperation - Africa-China Reporting Project*. Africa-China Reporting. https://africachinareporting.co.za/2015/11/impact-of-china-west-africa-healthcare-cooperation/

Shajalal, M., Xu, J., Jing, J., King, M., Zhang, J., Wang, P., . . . Cheng, F. (1970, January 1). *China's engagement with development assistance for health in Africa*. Global Health Research and Policy. https://ghrp.biomedcentral.com/articles/10.1186/s41256-017-0045-8

Shichor, Y. (2005, October 13). *Sudan: China's Outpost in Africa*. Jamestown. https://jamestown.org/program/sudan-chinas-outpost-in-africa/

Sun, Y. (2020, June 9). *China's debt relief for Africa: Emerging deliberations*. Brookings. https://www.brookings.edu/blog/africa-in-focus/2020/06/09/chinas-debt-relief-for-africa-emerging-deliberations/

Tambo, E., Ugwu, C. E., Guan, Y., & Wei, D. (2016). China-Africa Health Development Initiatives: Benefits and Implications for Shaping Innovative and Evidence-informed National Health Policies and Programs in Sub-saharan African Countries. *International Journal of MCH and AIDS*. https://www.ncbi.nlm.nih.gov/pmc/articles/PMC5187644/

Taylor, I. (2005, October 13). *Beijing's arms and oil interests in Africa*. Jamestown. https://jamestown.org/program/beijings-arms-and-oil-interests-in-africa/

Tesha, F. (2017, April 29). *China's Health Aid to Africa*. DukeSpace. https://dukespace.lib.duke.edu/dspace/handle/10161/14215

Thompson, D. (2005, October 13). *China's soft power in Africa: From the "Beijing consensus" to health diplomacy*. Jamestown. https://jamestown.org/program/chinas-soft-power-in-africa-from-the-beijing-consensus-to-health-diplomacy/

Wang, L., & Bateman, J. (2018, March 14). *China's Medical Aid in Africa*. The Diplomat. https://thediplomat.com/2018/03/chinas-medical-aid-in-africa/

Wang, X., & Sun, T. (2014, June). *China's engagement in global health governance: A critical analysis of China's assistance to the health sector of Africa*. http://www.jogh.org/documents/issue201401/V1_Wang.pdf

Weng, L., Sayer, J. A., & Xue, L. (2017, April 24). *Will China redefine development patterns in Africa? Evidence from Cameroon*. The Extractive Industries and Society. https://www.sciencedirect.com/science/article/pii/S2214790X16302301

Xia, Z.-G., Wang, R.-B., Wang, D.-Q., Feng, J., Zheng, Q., Deng, C.-S., . . . Xiao, N. (2014, December 2). *China–Africa Cooperation Initiatives in Malaria Control and Elimination*. Advances in Parasitology. https://www.sciencedirect.com/science/article/pii/B9780128008690000123

Xu, J., Yu, Q., Tchuenté, L.-A. T., Bergquist, R., Sacko, M., Utzinger, J., . . . Zhou, X.-N. (2016, March). Enhancing collaboration between China and African countries for schistosomiasis control. *The Lancet. Infectious diseases*. https://www.ncbi.nlm.nih.gov/pubmed/26851829

Yang, H.-M., Liu, P.-L., & Guo, Y. (2018, December 19). *Determinants of China's development assistance for health at the sub-national level of African countries (2006-2015)*. Infectious diseases of poverty. https://pubmed.ncbi.nlm.nih.gov/30587238/

Youde, J. (2010, March). *China's Health Diplomacy in Africa - ResearchGate*. ResearchGate. https://www.researchgate.net/publication/247827015_China's_Health_Diplomacy_in_Africa

Zhang, Y., Zhang, Y., & Guyatt, G. H. (2015, April 16). *Why West Africa rejected donation of Chinese medicine for treating Ebola recommended by Chinese government?* Complementary therapies in medicine. https://www.ncbi.nlm.nih.gov/pubmed/26051586/

Chapter 6
Current State of Chinese and USA Healthcare and Corona Care (COVID-19) in Africa

ABSTRACT

As Chinese and African countries grow in trade and economic development so has the soft power dynamics. Healthcare has been an area where the Chinese have dominated the area for the last decade. The USA has been in a decline and has been absent in providing the leadership in healthcare soft power dynamics. The partisan politics in the USA has consumed the United States Agency for International Development bringing an era of Chinese experimentation with a free market (capitalism) and toying with international development superpower status. Yet, there are still areas of improvement for healthcare in Africa between United States America (USA) and China (PRC). Africans have become used to engaging with the Chinese in the hope of meeting their developmental healthcare goals. But the acceptance of the Chinese healthcare and medicine in Africa is a game changer in the healthcare diplomacy arena.

INTRODUCTION

There exists friction in the partnership between China (PRC) and African Countries (the latter of which have shown their reliance to the point of agreeing to finance and land grants that are only beneficial to China) (Edeh et. al, 2021).

DOI: 10.4018/978-1-7998-4450-1.ch006

With regards to African Professionals, "the equivalent of 1 physician per day has migrated to the United States over the last decade"(Edeh et al, 2021; Mo Ibrahim foundation, 2018), thus reducing the number of providers who are available to offer services and engender wellness and health care practices. These issues (lack of appropriate financing and personnel) illustrate areas requiring improvement for appropriate health care on the African Continent. One solution is the acceptance of Chinese health care providers and medicine (traditional and western) in Africa.

In February of 2020, as a response to the COVID-19 pandemic, the African Center for Disease Control (CDC) established three goals which were "to limit transmission, limit deaths, and limit social and economic harms and impacts on other endemic diseases"(Maeda & Nkengasong, 2021). According to Maeda and Nkengasong (2021), the Africa Taskforce on Coronavirus (AFTCOR), with the complete support of the Bureau of Heads of State and Governments of the African Union, was developed and tasked with the execution of those goals. African health care organizations are the venues for addressing these goals.

Uganda

The China-Uganda Friendship Hospital Naguru (CUFH-N), which was built and donated by the Government of the People's Republic to the Government of Uganda on 6th January 2012 (P. 40, Chap. 3), has been the center of health care support and management for this global pandemic in Uganda. The goal of the hospital was to decongest Mulago National Referral Hospital, the only general public hospital serving an estimated 3 million inhabitants of the Kampala Metropolitan Area and has been very successful. The CUFH-N has had a vision of being a center of excellence in providing specialized and general health services.

Figure 1.

Benin

GRAND POPO, Benin, Sept. 19 (Xia, 2019) ten Chinese medical professionals of different specialties began a two-day mission to provide free health care services for the people of Grand Popo, about 100 km southwest of Benin's largest city Cotonou. "As part of celebrations marking the 70th anniversary of the founding of the People's Republic of China, the Chinese embassy in Benin had initiated free medical consultations for the benefit of the people of Grand Popo," Chinese Ambassador to Benin Peng Jingtao said. The medical team provided multiple health services in gynecology-obstetrics, otolaryngology, ophthalmology, stomatology, surgery, orthopedics, radiology, general medicine, pediatric, anesthesia and reanimation (Xia, 2019).

Cameroon

Forty years ago, Cameroon and China embarked on south-south cooperation. Since then, positive statistics have been recorded at Cameroon's Ministry of Public Health. For instance, between 1965-2015, over one million Cameroonians have been treated by the Chinese and acupuncture successfully practiced on close to 250,000 people in the four major Chinese hospitals in Cameroon (Xinhua, 2019). There are four major Chinese hospital/clinic in the Republic of Cameroon. These Chinese clinics/hospitals are the Chinese hospital in Douala, Hospital gyneco-obstetrique et Pediatrique de Ngousso Hospital Yaounde, Mbalmayo and Limbe respectively.

Figure 2.

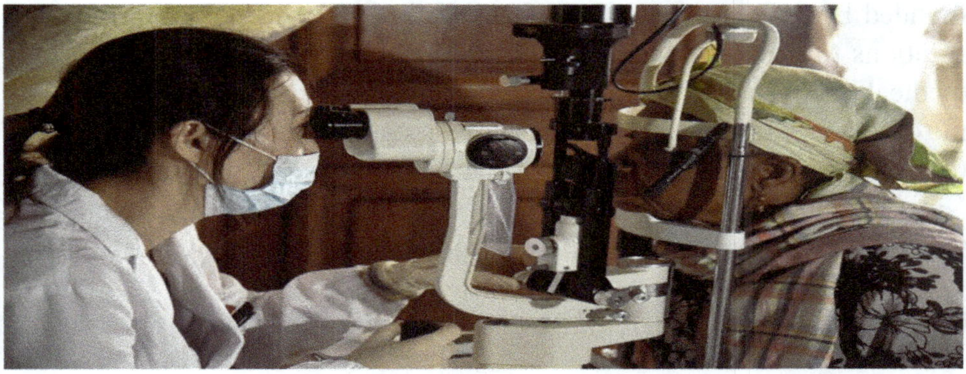

A Cameroonian resident receives free medical check in Mbalmayo, Cameroon, Aug. 3, 2019. (Photo by Jean Pierre Kepseu/Xinhua) By Arison Tamfu.

Tamfu (2019) YAOUNDE, Aug. 18 (Xinhua, 2019) on the eve of the arrival of a medical team with free services, villagers gathered in groups of twos and threes, buzzing with tales of the wondrous Chinese doctors. "Without them, I would have been dead" said Christophe Ndi Owona, the 76-year-old chief of the southern Cameroonian village of Ngat-Bane. Owona claims he had been suffering from severe headache for years. "Everybody thought I would die."

The team gave him medicine and advised him to stop drinking alcohol. "Thanks to the Chinese, I am now as healthy as a baby." The image of the Chinese and Chinese health care in Chinese has been instrumental in building the health care confident level of the local while increasing Chinese soft power.

Nigeria

According to a 2014 BBC World Service Poll, 80% of Nigerians view China's influence positively, with only 10% expressing a negative view, making Nigeria the most pro-Chinese nation in the world. There are three major Chinese operation in Nigeria, Chinese Natural Therapies (CNT) Medicare acupuncture & mire, Nyanya general hospital, and Okpeifa Herbal doctor. Saliu (Xinhua, 2019) stated tucked inside a vast residential area in the Jabi district of Abuja, the capital city of Nigeria, the first officially registered medical clinic in this West African country offers integrative medicine to local patients, incorporating traditional Chinese medicine, U.S. alternative medicine and Western medicine.

The health facility, named the Eastern and Western Hospital, was founded by a Chinese couple in 2017. This facility to provided adequate solutions to people's health problems by embracing Eastern and Western medical treatments. The hospital offers acupuncture and other CNT such as moxibustion, vacuum cupping, medical massage, chiropractic adjustment and Chinese herbal medicines. Most of the facilities are on the mainstream in Nigeria society hence, the acceptance of CNT has been used to accommodate Chinese superpower status in the most populous country in Africa.

Ghana

In (Xinhua, 2019) a newest batch of China-aided medical supplies was delivered to Ghana's Ledzokuku-Krowor Municipal (LEKMA) Hospital. The medical supplies worth 901,000 Chinese yuan (128,000 U.S. dollars) include a variety of equipment ranging from respirators to wheelchairs. Akua Afriyie Gyimah-Asante, director of the LEKMA hospital, also known as the China-Ghana Friendship Hospital, lauded China's long-term support for Ghana's medical and health services. China has sent eight batches of medical teams to Ghana in the past years. Besides working together with local doctors in the LEKMA Hospital, Chinese doctors also offer free services to locals in the country's remote areas.

In Chinese Traditional Medicine

According to (Chinagate, 2009) the director of the hospital, 41-year-old Xu Qinwei, decided to come to Ghana to open a hospital after his brother, a famous herbal doctor in Shandong Province in Eastern China, successfully cured an invited Ghanaian "Nana", one city chief in Ghana. The Nana suffered from serious cerebral infarction during the first Ministerial Conference of the Forum on China-Africa Cooperation in 2000. The Nana later invited his Chinese doctor for several times to open a hospital in Ghana. The hospital finally opened in early 2010 in Accra. Today, it has altogether 21 medical personnel including four Chinese doctors, with more than 50 local patients each day.

Here some of the major Chinese health care operation in Ghana:

1. Loving Life Chinese Clinic Hospital Accra, Ghana
2. 中国诊所 Chinese Acupuncture Clinic/Hospital Accra, Ghana

3. Prolife Chinese Acupuncture Clinic Hospital Ogbodjo, Ghana
4. Chinese Medical Team(中国医疗队Hospital Accra Beijing Clinic/ Hospital Accra, Ghana
5. China Natural Herbal Clinic Chinese medicine clinic
6. New East Chinese Hospital Kumasi
7. Loving Life Chinese Clinic Takorady

Kenya

Built by China Jiangxi International Economic and Technical Cooperation Co Ltd, the hospital is the first project totally financed by a Chinese concessional loan in Kenya totaling $104 million. The state-of-the-art facility, sitting on 100 acres of land about 45 minutes' drive from downtown Nairobi, has a capacity of 650 beds, including a 21-bed ICU and a 10-bed HDU (High Dependence Unit). It also boasts of specialized equipment, with a medical linear accelerator machine in the oncology department (China daily, 2019).

MOMBASA, Kenya—In 2007, the Bill & Melinda Gates Foundation said it was committed to eradicating malaria across the globe. By then, it was late to the game. That year, Chinese scientists working with a Chinese philanthropist and his company, New South, had already begun eradicating malaria from the small African nation of Comoros. Now they're setting their sights on a more ambitious location: Kenya, the East African nation of nearly 50 million people (Xinhua, 2019).

As Western donors garner headlines for funding expensive, experimental malaria interventions, Chinese researchers are undertaking a far more tested approach. Called mass drug administration, or MDA, it involves giving antimalarial pills to every man, woman, and child in each area all at once. Rather than kill off the world's mosquitoes, which spread the disease by drawing blood from infected people, the thinking goes, why not simply wipe out malaria among humans? These eradication approaches are completely different form the western medical approach (Kushner, 2019).

If successful, the effort would ease the disease's burden on Kenya's health system and economy. These successes will really catapult the Chinese medical technics and MDA across Africa. But it would also showcase Chinese philanthropy in Africa and may even help change the perception here that Chinese-made goods and medicine are of poor quality. Having recently surpassed the United States to become Africa's leading trade partner, and with Chinese investment in Africa rising sixtyfold from $500 million to $32 billion in the last 15 years, Chinese cooperation in the continent's science and public-health sectors may show the world that the country has far more to offer Africa than just roads, railways, and things (Kusher, 2019).

China has employed MDA, along with other methods to fight malaria, at home since at least 1981; last year, for the first time in what is likely millennia, it saw no new native cases of the disease. But MDA is controversial for reasons of both science and ethics. There are concerns that it could lead to increased drug resistance, which could see malaria rise to levels not seen in decades. Others believe it's unethical to give antimalarials to people who may not even have the disease—or who don't wish to take them—though such qualms are dismissed in Kenya and elsewhere. Similar dilemmas are challenging U.S. policy makers as they debate how to respond to the rising anti-vax movement (Kusher, 2019).

Guo (2019; Xinhua, 2019) economic and commercial counselor of Chinese Embassy in Kenya, said during the handover ceremony in Nairobi that the Kenyatta University Teaching Referral and Research Hospital is the first hospital project fully financed by Chinese concessional loan. "It has been equipped with the world-class medical facilities which are rare not only in Kenya but also in China," said Guo.

The hospital was built by China Jiangxi International Economic and Technical Cooperation Co., Ltd. These reliable development partner and true friend, the Chinese government cooperates closely with the Kenyan side and has provided massive financial and technical support since 1960s, adding that the Chinese government has offered a lot of loan support to Kenya.

The Chinese envoy noted that half of all loans from China are on preferential export buyer credit and government concessional loans at low interest rates, which are just a quarter or even less than the prevailing international financial market rates. If these rates are true western lending institutions like the World Bank cannot match some of the rates and activities. Olive Mugenda, chairperson of Kenyatta University Teaching Referral and Research Hospital, said that the new modern hospital will complement the work of the two other existing referral hospitals in Kenya. Mugenda said that Kenyatta University Teaching Referral and Research Hospital will improve the lives of Kenyans through facilitating evidence-based health care in the country (Guo, 2019; Xinhua 2019).

According to the chairperson, the facility is expected to host the first breast cancer treatment facility in Kenya. Joseph Kinyua, head of public service, said that the state-of-the-art hospital will help Kenya achieve its strategy on universal healthcare. Kenya losses significant amount of foreign exchange when its citizens go abroad to search for medical treatment. "This hospital facility will help Kenya to reduce outbound medical tourism and promote inbound medical tourism from the rest of Africa," he added (Guo, 2019; Xinhua 2019).

The number of Kenyans leaving the country for specialized treatment is set to decline as a new specialized hospital prepares to open its doors soon in Nairobi. The Chinese-funded and -built Kenyatta University Teaching and Referral Hospital on Friday was handed over to the Kenyan government, which plans to commission it in two and a half months (China daily, 2019).

Figure 3.

Chinese migrants in Kenya fear visiting local hospitals for perceived poor care and high cost of services, shows a recent study in Nairobi and Kisumu. The migrants working or living in Kenya also fear being misdiagnosed or infected with diseases in local hospitals especially HIV.

"Some said they were concerned about the risk of acquiring infectious diseases such as HIV in Kenyan healthcare facilities," says the study published two weeks ago. Consequently, when they get sick, they treat themselves with medicines from home, seek Chinese Traditional Medicines in Kenya or travel back home (China Daily, 2019).

Kenya Pharmaceutics:

The China Chamber of Commerce for Import and Export of Medicines & Health Products (CCCMHPIE), held a trade and investment forum together with the Ministry of Health Kenya and the private health sector in Kenya on the 30th of August 2018 at the Laico Regency Hotel in Nairobi.

Figure 4.

Public and Private Health Sector Stakeholders During China – Kenya Pharmaceutical Trade and Investment Forum

According the (Kenya Pharmaceutical Trade and Investment, 2019) the main aim of the forum was to establish and maintain a good relationship between Kenyan and Chinese healthcare sectors and further explore investment opportunities in the Kenyan pharmaceutical industry. This forum was sponsored by UKAID and brought together participants from Ministry of Health Kenya, Pharmacy and Poisons Board Kenya, the Kenya Healthcare Federation, the Kenya Chamber of Commerce, the Economic & Commercial Counsellor's Office at the Embassy of the People's Republic of China, and the China Africa Friendship Association.

Ms. Guo Xiaodan deputy secretary of sub-chamber, department of pharmaceutical, CCCMHPIE, opened the forum by welcoming the guests. In her opening speech, she reiterated that she's extremely happy to visit Kenya and establish a lasting relationship between Kenyan and Chinese healthcare sectors.

CCCMHPIE was established in May in 1989. It is the most internationalized and influential healthcare industry association in China the key areas of responsibility include: policy and industry coordination, conferences and training, exhibitions registration, consulting, market surveys and analysis reports in traditional Chinese medicines, pharmaceuticals, medical devices & dressings, biopharmaceuticals and functional cosmetics (KPTI, 2019).

In his speech, Mr. Tan Shengcai, head of the Chinese healthcare delegation gave a background of Kenya – China relationship especially in investment. He emphasized that Kenya has been contracting China in building and construction particularly in road construction. There is need to have deeper engagement especially in the healthcare industry. He invited the Chinese healthcare delegates to evaluate the Kenyan market and see possible investment opportunities in the pharmaceutical industry (KPTI, 2019).

Malawi

According to Kadango (2020) the People's Republic of China has promised to construct a state-of-the-art health facility in Blantyre's North East Constituency, Malawi News Agency has learnt. The Chinese Ambassador to Malawi, Liu Hongyang, revealed the development when he visited the area Saturday to appreciate what the Chinese Medical team is doing to serve people's lives in the area.

Mozambique

MAPUTO, March 9 (Yi, 2020) Chinese medical team in Mozambique gave a lecture here on Friday on women's sexual and reproductive health to students and teachers in Mozambique's prestigious Eduardo Mondlane University.

"We had a small lecture about women's sexual and reproductive health. The doctors went through sexually transmitted diseases on how to prevent them. They spoke about the contraception methods, very important for women like us as college students," Gatina Isabel, a student and participant, told Xinhua.

Figure 5.

Figure 6.

Local people dance at a welcome ceremony held by the Mozambican side for the visiting Chinese naval hospital ship Peace Ark at the Maputo Port in Maputo, capital of Mozambique on Nov 7, 2017. (81.cn/Su Gang)

Mozambique is the 36th country the Peace Ark has visited since it joined the PLA Navy in 2008. Over 500 people including officials from the Mozambique Defense Ministry and Navy, working staff of the Chinese

Embassy in Mozambique, local overseas Chinese welcomed the Chinese naval hospital ship at the port (Shan, 2017).

Namibia

The outgoing 12th Chinese medical team pose for photos with Chinese and Namibian officials in Katutura State Hospital in Windhoek, capital of Namibia, on Jan. 16, 2020 (Xinhua, 2020)

The outgoing 12th Chinese medical team stationed in Namibia managed to administer Traditional Chinese Medicine (TCM) to over 20,000 patients during their one year and a half tenure at the Chinese Acupuncture Department of Katutura State Hospital as well as other facilities in the country (Xinhua, 2020). In area of the country that have been historically underserved the Chinese medical team provides need medical care for the all Namibia citizen regardless their financial capacity. These services have provided Chinese with a win win foreign policy in a country that is far from the eastern shore of Africa.

Togo

China, Togo Sign Handover Document of Local Hospital in Lome.

Togolese Health Minister Comlan Mally (L) and Chinese Ambassador to Togo Yang Min sign the handover document of the Lome Central Hospital in Lome, capital of Togo, on June 17, 2009, marking the completion of the civil engineering work of the building. The hospital, sponsored and built by Chinese government, covered an area of 5,934 square meters and would be completed at the end of the year 2009 [Xinhua].

According to China daily (2019) the 23rd Chinese medial team to Togo provided free consultations and healthcare to agricultural populations of Kpele-Akata, about 150 km northwest to the capital Lome. Initiated by the Chinese embassy in Togo, jointly with the cabinet of the Chairwoman of the National assembly of Togo, the free healthcare provision occurred in the medical and social center of Adeta, in southern Togo. The Chairwoman of the National assembly Chantal Yawa Tsegan witnessed healthcare provision and hailed Chinese health specialists for having mobilized to assist people of this highly agricultural activities area in southern Togo.

Figure 7.

The free healthcare campaign took place nearly a month after the 23rd Chinese medical team from Shanxi Province arrived in Lome on November 22 and started their work in the regional health center of Lome-Commune, a hospital center constructed by China as part of it cooperation with the African country. Approximately 300 people benefited from the free health campaign. “We are now ever conscious of the importance of the Chinese medical mission in Togo,” chief medical team Chen Haiyun told Xinhua. The 23rd Chinese medical team comprises ten specialists in general surgery, traumatology, general medicine, acupuncture, and gynecology and laboratory medicine. The medical cooperation is an important pillar of the bilateral cooperation following the establishment of diplomatic ties between the two countries since 1972 (Xinhua, 2019).

Rwanda

China donates medical supplies to Rwandan hospital

Director of Masaka Hospital Marcel Uwizeye (4th R, front), members of the 19th Chinese Medical Team in Rwanda and others pose for a group photo following a medical aids donation ceremony in Kigali, capital city of Rwanda, on May 29, 2019. The 19th Chinese Medical Team in Rwanda on Wednesday handed over medical aids to Masaka Hospital in Kigali. (Xinhua/ Wang Junbo)

Figure 8.

KIGALI, May 29 (Xinhua, 2019) The 19th Chinese Medical Team in Rwanda on Wednesday handed over medical aids to Masaka Hospital in the Rwandan capital city Kigali. The aids, donated by the Chinese government which entrusted the Chinese medical team to hand over, are selected in line with Masaka Hospital's need, the Chinese medical team told Xinhua after a donation ceremony held in the hospital built with financing by the Chinese government. The citizen of Rwanda a land locked country in central Africa is not except from the reach of soft power diplomacy from China.

Zambia

LUSAKA, May 14 (Xinhua, 2018) The Zambian government on Monday honored the 19th Chinese Medical Team for their exemplary work during their tour of duty in the southern African nation. All the 28 members of the team, who have been in Zambia since May last year, were presented with the awards during a ceremony attended by senior Zambian government officials as well as officials from the Chinese embassy. Chitalu Chilufya, Zambia's Minister of Health said the government was happy to honor the doctors who worked diligently to strengthen health systems in the country.

He said the doctors worked diligently during their tour of duty as evidenced in improved service delivery in the four hospitals where they were stationed in. Zambia and China, he said, have developed cordial relations in the last 40 years in the health sector which has resulted in the improvement of both infrastructure in the sector and capacity building of health personnel (Xinhua 2018).

Since 1978, China has dispatched a total of 515 doctors to Zambia, he added. The Chinese envoy said China has achieved remarkable progress in the health sector and was committed to work with Zambia to promote the country's medical and health industry. The Chinese medical team, he said, helped to train a group of high-level medical staffs in Zambia by clinical teaching, academic lectures, and mutual expert visits, which helped in bringing traditional Chinese medical treatment methods and advanced medical ideas (Xinhua, 2018).

Those growing worried include employees at the Sino-Zambia Friendship Hospital in the mining city of Kitwe in northern Zambia, near the Congo border. Chinese companies operate mines on the outskirts of the city of more than half a million people. One company is headquartered in Wuhan, the city at the center of the virus outbreak. Hundreds of workers traveled between Zambia and China in recent weeks. As the corona pandemic spread globally these Chinese health facilities have been a center of controversy. Wuhan the epicenter of the pandemic has a lot of worker in Zambia. The employees and others familiar with the matter, some of whom spoke anonymously under the new rules, say some Chinese patients checked in with coughs and fevers but did not get placed in isolation.

The Sino-Zambia Friendship Hospital, or Sinozam, a low-slung facility near the city's train station, has taken some precautions, including checking patient temperatures with infrared thermometers and establishing isolation areas. Employees wear masks. Gloves, disinfectant and oxygen inhalers have been stockpiled. Sinozam treats many Chinese in Kitwe and its precautions go further than other hospitals in the area. But there is still some element of truth between the local Zambia and the medical facility

REFERENCES

Africa, A. (2016). *China's Role in Improving Public Health in Cameroon*. Allafrica.com. https://allafrica.com/stories/201604290681.html

CCGN. (2020). *Chinese Medical Team in Namibia treats over 20000 patients in 18 months*. https://africa.cgtn.com/2020/01/17/chinese-medical-team-in-namibia-treats-over-20000-patients-in-18-months/

Chidiebere, E., Adekunle, O., Michael, M., Omoruyi, E., & Zhao, C. (2021). Bolstering African strategy for sustainable development and its diaspora's influence on African development renaissance. *Migration and Development*. doi:10.1080/21632324.2020.1855737

GuoS.JiangH. (2020). *Chinese Aid and Local Employment in Africa*. doi:10.2139srn.3718578

Jiechi, Y. (2013). *Magic Chinese Medicine in Ghanaian patients eyes Magical Chinese Medicine*. http://www.china.org.cn/world/Off_the_Wire/2013-01/23/content_27777423.htm

Jingyao, L. (2019). Chinese naval hospital ship Peace Ark arrives in Mozambique for visit. *China Military Online*.

KadangoL. (2020). https://allafrica.com/stories/201812100417.htm

Kang, D., Sichalwe, N., & Cara, A. (2020). *We are definitely not prepared: Africa brace for New virus*. Retrieved, March 21, 2020, from https://apnews.com/e11a9c5801264262e0b2f8661408b32a

KPTI China-Kenya pharmaceutical and investment forum. (2019). Retrieved, March 15, 2020 from http://khf.co.ke/china-kenya-pharmaceutical-trade-and-investment-forum/

Kusher, J. (2019). *China is leading the next step in fighting malaria in Africa*. https://www.theatlantic.com/international/archive/2019/07/china-tackles-malaria-kenya/592414/

Li, X. (2017). *China hands over 104 million dollar hospital to Kenya*. Retrieved, May 03 from http://www.xinhuanet.com/english/2019-05/24/c_138086768.htm

Maeda, J., & Nkengasong, J. (2021). The puzzle of the COVID-19 pandemic in Africa. *Science*, *1*, 27–28.

Mo Ibrahim Foundation. (2018). *Brain drain: A bane to Africa's potential*. Mo Ibrahim Foundation Report. https://mo.ibrahim.foundation/news/2018/brain-drain-bane-africas-potential#:~:text=Brain%20drain%2C%20which%20is%20the,emigrate%20from%20Africa%20every%20y

Oloo, M. (2020). *Why Chinese who live in Kenya fear local hospital*. Retrieved, March 23, 2020 From,https://www.standardmedia.co.ke/health/article/2001355244/why-chinese-who-live-in-kenya-fear-local-hospitals

Saliu, O. (2019). *East Meets West as traditional Chinese Medicine become popular in Nigeria*. http://www.xinhuanet.com/english/2019-03/15/c_137898085.htm

Shan, J. (2017). *Chinese naval hospital ship peace ark arrives in Mozambique*. Retrieved, March 22, 2020 from http://eng.mod.gov.cn/news/2017-11/08/content_4796910.htm

Tamfu, A. (2019). *Chinese medical team provides free treatment in rural Cameroon*. Retrieved, March 10 2020, from http://www.xinhuanet.com/english/2019-08/18/c_138318534.htm

Uganda, Ministry to Health. (n.d.). *China-Uganda friendship Hospital*. Retrieved, March, 16 2020 https://health.go.ug/content/china-uganda-friendship-hospital-naguru

Xia, L. (2019). *Chinese medical team provides free health services in Benin town*. Retrieved, March 20, 2020, from http://www.xinhuanet.com/english/2019-09/20/c_138407390.htm

Xinhua. (2019a). *Chinese medical team provides free healthcare in southern Togo*. Retrieved May 14, 2020, from https://www.chinadaily.com.cn/a/201912/29/WS5e08c4c3a310cf3e355814c0.html

Xinhua. (2019b). *Chinese to go sign handover document of local hospital in Lome*. http://en.chinagate.cn/photos/2009-06/19/content_17979740.htm

Xinhua. (2019c). *China donates medical supplies for Rwanda Hospital*. Retrieved, March 15, 2021, from http://www.xinhuanet.com/english/2019-05/30/c_138100882.htm

Xinhua. (2020). *Zambia Honor Chinese medical team for exemplary work*. Retrieved, Feb 20, 2021, from http://www.xinhuanet.com/english/2018-05/15/c_137178980.htm

Chapter 7
The State of International Healthcare Development in Africa

ABSTRACT

An estimated 1 million Chinese live and work in Africa. The interaction between Chinese and Native Africans is correlated with the increase in Chinese commerce on the African continent. However, a number of these interactions were not friendly. Many of the Chinese now face added scrutiny or outright discrimination due to their treatment of Native Africans as depicted in social media. The discord between USAID and the Chinese Government has negatively impacted the state of international healthcare development in Africa. Healthy debate and the implementation of collaborative solutions have been compromised by social media discrimination images. Non-traditional media has led the debate on the soft power control of Africa. This chapter explores the state of international healthcare development in Africa.

COVID-19

Covid-19 is at pandemic levels worldwide. Still the continent of Africa, at the time of their document, was the least affected with less than 300 reported cases in its 54 countries. As these cases rise, a new and difficult health issue will have to be addressed, as well as the biases that accompany it.

DOI: 10.4018/978-1-7998-4450-1.ch007

Adede, et al. (2020) reports on the Voice of America (VOA) that as the coronavirus spreads across continents, it is also spreading fear. In many parts of the world, including Africa, xenophobia, and more specifically, "sinophobia," the fear of Chinese people, is on the rise. An estimated 1 million Chinese live and work in Africa. Many now face added scrutiny or outright discrimination. Chinese have immigrated to every country on the continent. As the business has increased, between Chinese and Africans, so has the interaction between the two ethnic groups. Some of these interactions as mentioned earlier have not been friendly.

According to Penny (2020), as the novel coronavirus rages through the world and spreads rapidly in the U.S., Africa is the least-affected continent at the moment, with less than 300 reported cases in roughly half of its 54 countries so far. Many media outlets have reacted with a confounded tone, surprised that Africa does not have more cases and are wondering if the low numbers are due to a lack of testing. Regional experts say a widespread pandemic in Africa could cripple the continent's fragile health-care systems and be devastating economically. It also could be difficult to contain while foreign donor nations that traditionally assist the continent in such crises are overwhelmed with their outbreaks (Penny, 2020).

One question in Africa is whether the number of confirmed cases is so low simply because the virus isn't being detected. At the beginning of February only two countries in sub-Saharan Africa —Senegal and South Africa — could test for the novel coronavirus. WHO has helped 43 more countries set up or augment their national laboratories so that they can also test for this pathogen (National Public Radio NPR, 2020). Many analysts are puzzled by this trend given that several African countries have strong trade and travel ties with China. These countries might have been worried about the COVID-19 coming into their borders with the Chinese AID workers. Some as mention earlier had started fighting against Sino-phobia that had been developing because of conspiracy theories and fake news about COVID-19.

While it's still not clear why so few cases in Africa emanated from the Asian country, some have attributed this to either a lack of reporting of cases or effective border screening. But according to the Chinese government, this is down to tightened measures to limit any further exportation of the new coronavirus (COVID-19) to Africa and other regions by learning from "experience." (Motambo, 2020).

Africa as a Global Health Link

The pandemic is exposing major flaws in higher-income countries' health systems and turning the tables on decades of travel restrictions targeting Africans. When West Africa suffered from the Ebola crisis from 2014 to 2016, the region was often painted as a weak link in the global health system, and many airlines cut flights to Guinea, Liberia, and Sierra Leone. Four years later, Africa is at risk of contamination primarily from Europe, China, and the U.S. Besides Egypt, nearly all the continent's confirmed cases have come from travelers from European or East Asian countries, though that looks likely to change soon as cases rise rapidly across the continent and community transmission becomes more likely (Penny, 2020). There were still flights coming in African countries while some European, Asia and Americas countries had reduced or stop flights.

According to (Xinhua, 2018) in 2015, the Forum on China-Africa Cooperation summit in Johannesburg listed public health cooperation as part of the 10 China-Africa cooperation plans, lifting China-Africa health cooperation to a new level. China and Africa have also seen deepened cooperation in the health sector thanks to efforts from both sides in recent years. Besides, medical service such as China-led Brightness Action campaign and medical training has also witnessed achievements.

Republic of Congo

In the Republic of Congo, since the China-led Brightness Action campaign was launched in 2016, the China-Congo Friendship Hospital (CCFH), where the Chinese medical team in the country is stationed, has been receiving modern surgical supplies and medical instruments from China to treat eye illness. Zhang Weipeng, an ophthalmologist at the hospital and the doctor in charge of cataract surgery, said his department receives an average of 30 patients every day and many of them come to CCFH specialty for phacoemulsification (Xinhua, 2018).

South Africa

In earlier (2020), when the first reports of the coronavirus started to come out of China, global health officials said they were very worried about what would happen if the virus started spreading in Africa, where many health systems are already struggling (Penny 2020). According to the Nation Public Radio (NPR) as of March 21, 2020, more than half the nations on the continent 36 of the 54 countries — had reported cases. South Africa, with 150 cases, is the only one with more than 100. Nonetheless, many countries in Africa are responding aggressively to the pandemic. Schools were ordered closed in the Nigerian capital of Lagos after only eight cases were confirmed nationwide. Last week South Africa banned visitors from high-risk countries, closed schools, and quickly opened drive-through testing centers in Johannesburg.

In South Africa (Richie, 2020) the Chinese ambassador to South Africa, Lin Songtian, pushed back against suggestions his country should carry sole responsibility for COVID-19, saying while the globally-spreading disease was first reported in its city, Wuhan, there was no evidence it had originated there. But most African without any doubt have associated the COVID-19 with China. There is not limited to one million Chinese living in the Africa Continents. South Africa was one of the first countries in the Africa Continent to close its borders. But they were still willing to bring back their fellow citizen infected with the virus. Building trust between the South African government and its citizens was the best way to overcome COVID-19.

According to Motambo (2020), the World Health Organization recently declared Europe the new epicenter of the virus, with Italy first going on complete lockdown because they had been hardest hit. Some African countries have sent back European citizens by refusing entry. Due to the political gravitas of the People's Republic of China, most china citizens were advised to quarantine for fourteen days. Refusing entry from Chinese citizens could be detrimental to the local and the national economy. Although China has reported most cases of the virus, it has had a lower death rate compared to Italy, Iran, Spain, and Germany.

While President Trump has referred on numerous occasions that the coronavirus is Chinese. Chinese officials in Beijing have decried calling the virus the Chinese virus. These United States officials haven't been able to trace how the virus jumped to other countries. But the few cases African nations have reported in Africa had not to be linked directly to China. The Chinese government has been trying to reduce the impact of these country-to-country infections by implementing a travel ban. In eastern Africa, only the Somalia coronavirus case was linked directly from Asia. Ethiopia, Kenya, Tanzania, Rwanda, and Sudan have all been reported, mostly from passengers who came in from Europe, the US, or the United Arab Emirates (Motambo, 2020).

Penny (2020) the U.S.'s failure to prepare adequately for the spread of COVID-19, and the confused messaging from Donald Trump, has meant the U.S. is a weak link in the world health system, making it more difficult to fight the disease globally. "I expected America to stand strong against this pandemic, but they failed the world — that's my clear assessment," an Ethiopian health official, who asked not to be named, told The Intercept. "The international community should stand in solidarity" but instead the pandemic was viewed initially as China's loss and America's gain. These geopolitical games in health care have only increased and created more problems for the pandemic than solutions and Africa for once is not the center of the pandemic.

Ghana

Paterson's (2020) research in Ghana shows patients may question medical approaches to health issues with "unseen" causes such as mental health disorders. A lack of confidence in public health services is one reason people with chronic conditions such as mental health disorders delay seeking care. Even with this delay acknowledged in the health care system of most African countries they might still be more prepared because of the recent Ebola epidemic. (Penny, 2020) Africa's strong response might not be able to hold on for much longer, however, as new cases have shown up in Ghana, Gabon, Guinea, Rwanda, and Kenya. Sudan's first case tested positive posthumously, indicating that the disease was already there and spreading unchecked for multiple weeks.

Patterson (2020) reported studies on race and health in the United States and global immunization campaigns to indicate that trust is an all-important element. Without trust, people tend not to heed health information or follow treatment advice. There are historical events that support this element of trust in the United States Public Health system at home and abroad. Distrust of public health institutions meant people avoided health-care centers during West Africa's 2014-2016 Ebola outbreak, for instance. The breeding of misinformation and disinformation is the source of health care distrust in these communities.

Corruption within public services deepens people's suspicions of government health actions, and it undermines health-care access. When new diseases such as Ebola in West Africa or COVID-19 emerge, a lack of scientific knowledge or patient personal experience also can undermine confidence in health-care institutions Paterson (2020). The arrogance of foreign media to attribute corruption in undermining confidence in the health care system is out-weigh by the way fiscal support is allocated to these countries. Both the Chinese and the United States have failed in the allocation of financial support as international development.

The Chinese have been criticized for bringing too much labor from china, offering higher interest rate loans, and not building a bond with local communities. Their main contacts have been the ministry and top government officials. International development even in health care is supposed to create jobs for local individuals so, that the local health care system can be built kept and maintain capacity. Contrary, the United States has been the focus on a top-down approach in meeting the needs of these developing African countries. They have left the ground approach to a non-governmental organization (NGO) which has become an even bigger source of employment in the United States not for African as well. This ground game approach has been a failure for the United States to meet the needs of these African partner countries.

According to the United States Agency for International Development (USAID) (2018) in the average salary was $102,785. This is 66.8 percent higher than the national average for government employees and 56.3 percent higher than other federal agencies. A Guardian (2016, March) articles acknowledge the hypocrisy in aid agencies coming to the developing country looking to improve local lives, yet economically discriminate against local staff within their organization. Local staff is seen more as tools to implement aid programs without the expertise to make the big decisions. But local staff have knowledge that cannot be learned at any institution and many are highly educated with years of experience. The highest-paid local employee receives less than the international intern in the renowned UN program.

A local western-educated aid worker at an international humanitarian NGO in an East African country negotiated hard for my salary of over $1,500 (£1,000) a month, making him one of the highest-paid local staff. While developmental health jobs in the United States are paid ten (10) to fifteen (15) times more than the average African health care developmental employees. According to the United States Agency for International Development (USAID) in 2018, the average salary was $102,785.

The international development health care industry incorporates a lot of Americans on these development projects which the salary discrimination leads to a lack of mutual trust. The lack of trust brings great inefficiency in building developmental health care strategies and goodwill. The combatting of a pandemic with mistrust can be a major vehicle for vicious rumors and conspiracy theories as most of the workers are not locals. A good example of this health care mistrust and conspiracy theory is the Ebola Crisis in West and Central Africa. These mistrust issues make success in some of these projects more difficult to achieve and eventually costing more African lives and the superpower image of the United States.

We the United States (USAID) should stop operating like the World Bank or other funding institutions. Our goodwill strategy should be implemented from the bottom up with more Africans involved in these projects than Americans. We are no different from the Chinese when we bring in more employees for a health care goodwill mission than the locals. The locals should be paid well. A complete and total reduction of American should eventually be our greatest asset in these projects. We should think about the African leading some of these projects and we provide technical and financial support as requested by our partners the Africans. We should not only initiate these projects but should develop, maintain, operations to ensure program continuity by hiring more locals. These programs should not be stopped because of a lack of funding nor the new policy or ideology of the new president. International health care development should be free from U.S. politics.

Institutional Foundation Chinese

Chinese billionaire and co-founder of Alibaba, Jack Ma, says he will donate masks, test kits, and protective suits to all countries in Africa to help the continent in its fight against the novel coronavirus. Ma's foundation will donate a total of 1.1 million testing kits, six million masks, and 60,000 protective suits and face shields. They will also work with local medical institutions on the continent to provide online training material for coronavirus clinical treatments (Patrick, 2020). The Chinese have developed a better system by letting locals operate and manage the COVID-19 crisis in collaboration with private Chinese firms like the Jack Ma Foundations. These foundations like all entity in Chinese is highly influenced by the Chinese Central Government.

Penny (2020) unlike the U.S., where the Centers for Disease Control and Prevention reportedly blocked testing of the virus while spreading at a nursing home in Washington state, and has struggled to provide an adequate response across the nation. There is strong political will from countries like Senegal to ensure that concerned citizens have access to tests. These efforts have been replicated across Africa without direct health from the United States like the Ebola crisis.

Senegal

Senegal, which is currently getting test kits from WHO, and plans to manufacture its testing kits with support from the U.K., which will be ready by June. Dr. Amadou Sall, the director of Senegal's Institute Pasteur, has been responsible for testing in the country (Richie, 2020). "I'm happy and proud what Africa has done this time because usually, we spend time running after epidemics when it is there, but at this time we have been prepared." African countries are working closely with the WHO, a global body from which the Trump administration has tried to cut 65 million dollars. The U.S. decided not to use WHO's kits, according to Dr. Ashish Jha, a director of Harvard University's Global Health Institute.

The failure of the United States to lead in this pandemic has left a void in the global health community. There was an opportunity for the Trump administration to present his make America great again policies in the international development arena. His failure to make America great again in the international global health arena will have detrimental consequences in the future. The developmental strategy of the whole western nations not only the United States' status as a world leader will be in serious doubt. In the global battle of the COVID-19, the United States has shown cracks in the health care systems while the Chinese have prevailed in public opinion. China has set up hospitals and shut down major metropolitan areas while the United States' approaches have been haphazard. There has been great confusion in the policies and implementation goals to slow-down COVID-19 in the United States.

Ethiopian

The World Health Organization chief, Tedros Adhanom Ghebreyesus, was responding at the end of last month to cases of anti-Chinese prejudice. He repeated the message on Twitter earlier this week while sharing a story about a Singaporean man who was beaten up in the UK capital, London, over the coronavirus. Ethiopia's first case, was a Japanese man coming from Burkina Faso, making it the first case of cross-continental transmission. It also means there are likely more unreported cases in Burkina Faso, which does not have the resources that Senegal has and is fighting an insurgency that has crippled its state (Penny, 2020).

Kenya

According to Mwaura (2020) before Kenya has even recorded a case, the fear, mixed with stigma, is palpable. Kenya is not alone in this prejudice, but what is interesting is that all the initial cases of the virus in sub-Saharan Africa have been linked to European travel rather than China. Yet there is no equivalent anti-European feeling. Kenyans have campaigned to stop flights coming in from China. The prejudice has been fueled by China and Kenya's entwined economic relationship. The virus of prejudice is spreading and Kenya is no exception.

Mwaura also indicated that on 27 February stated, a message went viral on Facebook, allegedly posted by a Kenyan member of parliament, calling for his constituency residents to avoid interaction with Chinese nationals who had just returned from China after celebrating their new year (2020). The post warned that if the government did not do enough to protect its citizens, and forcefully quarantine any of these Chinese nationals, then the residents had his permission to chase away and stone any Chinese people within their vicinity. China's embassy responded quickly with a Twitter post calling for a "rational and scientific approach towards Chinese communities" and described the remarks that had been made as racist.

Liberia

Kaiman (2014). China plans to build a 100-bed medical center in Liberia to combat Ebola, after criticism that they were not doing enough to fight the disease. The Chinese foreign ministry sent 1,000 aid workers to Ebola-affected areas and has already sent 252 people to the three hardest-hit countries – Guinea, Liberia, and Sierra Leone (Xinhua, 2014). Foreign ministry spokesman Hong Lei elaborated on the in Liberia, they have built a 100-bed medical center, 160 medical workers were already going there, and 320 additional workers would arrive at the center at a later date.

Investing in Diplomacy

According to Xia (2018), the Chinese have called for intensified efforts to improve the accessibility of Africa's health services, strengthen the public health prevention and control system and capacity-building in Africa, scale-up support for the health needs of the youth and women, deepen people-to-people exchanges in health and bring more benefits to the people through China-Africa health cooperation. While the United States under President Donald Trump is having a policy of “America first”. We the United States need to develop a Policy of America global Equity which I will refer to as Eyombo’s Law of International Health Equity (ELIHE).

ELIHE states an increase in development health equity will increase economic development, strengthen international diplomacy and societal goodwill. The United States is on the global field and if they do not play the Chinese will. The analogy of soccer games and players partaking in the games results in a win or loss for the United States. The lack of a United States health care team in the international health development arena while focusing on “American first” has been forfeiting their games to the People Republic of China. Africa is the most important strategic playground for global health and equity in redefining the United States’ strategic goodwill.

Africa yearns to seek a leadership and development partnership that has been enhanced by the new social media generation. The admiration of the United States as a fair broker economically will bring social equity through the support of good governance. The expectation of Africa’s generation X, Y, and Z will be in full support with most of these health programs. Strong men, despots, and dictators should be completely discouraged by been supportive of true democratically elected governments. COVID-19 should be a game where the United States should take the leadership mantle and define the rules of the games while increasing our diplomatic goodwill and global strength.

Mcdowell & Donohue (2019) note that book value and market value won’t necessarily be the same thing. Diplomatic market value is the maximum value of the United States in optimizing developmental institutions like health care to increase international confidence in our systems of government. In Financial terms, book value depends solely upon the company’s reported financial condition, while market value is primarily based upon the company’s cash flow and the public’s confidence in how the company will do in the future. Our market value diplomacy is affected by the perception of public confidence in these African countries.

The difference between market value and book value is goodwill. Our goodwill globally needs to be in excess, as our market value after the Second World War. Everything American was good and we stood for what was right and exercised great moral values. The absence of the United States on the playground for COVID-19 has lower the expectation of African and reduce this global health equity. Even though the United States has past extended goodwill, failure to lead the COVID-19 pandemic has reduced our diplomatic market value.

The two values can be the same, close to the same, or quite far apart. If the book value of a company is more than the market value, it could mean that public interest or confidence in the company or its industry might not be as high. Now with the "America First" description of the United States, our international interest and confidence are low. If the market value is higher than the book value, the public may expect the company or industry to take off (McDowell and Donohue, 2019). We need to get into the international Development games to increase our market values and international public confidence.

The absence of the United States on the playing field for COVID-19 has been bad but the Chinese have done worst in the African court of public opinion. Asiedu (2020) indicated that across African capitals, Chinese Ambassadors are being hauled over by foreign ministries to explain horrid scenes that have gone viral on social media platforms of African migrants being evicted from their apartments and refused entry into hotels. The Chinese local government has evicted people of African descent from their house in the Southern China town of Guangzhou. This has been a turning point in the corona pandemic. The Chinese claim they are preventing the reoccurrence of the COVID-19, but the Africans see this as total racism. The Africans claim they did not treat the Chinese the same way they are been treated in Guangzhou. Even though there is no dispute this corona pandemic started in the Chinese. There are numerous videos on Facebook and WhatsApp going viral with people of African descent being evicted from their house in Guangzhou, China. Here is the opportunity for the United States to make American International health development policy great again.

REFERENCES

Adede, C. L., Chombo, A., & Kaseko, O. (2020, March 21). Retrieved May 01, 2020, from https://www.voanews.com/science-health/coronavirus-outbreak/coronavirus-brings-sinophobia-africa https://www.npr.org/sections/goatsandsoda/2020/03/21/818894991/african-countries-respond-quickly-to-spread-of-covid-19

Asiedu, G. K. (2020, April 11). *After enduring months of lockdown, Africans in China are being targeted and evicted from apartments*. Quartz Africa. Retrieved from March 9, 2021. https://qz.com/africa/1836510/africans-in-china-being-evicted-from-homes-after-lockdown-ends/

French, H. (2014). *China's Second Continent: How a Million Migrants Are Building a New Empire in Africa*. Knopf.

Guardian. (2016). *Secret aid worker: Why do ex-pats earn more than the rest of the US?* Retrieved, March 18, 2021, from https://www.theguardian.com/global-development-professionals-network/2016/mar/29/secret-aid-worker-why-do-expats-earn-more-than-the-rest-of-us

Kaiman, J. (2014, November 6). *China to build Ebola hospital in Liberia*. Retrieved March 9, 2021, from https://www.theguardian.com/world/2014/nov/06/china-build-ebola-hospital-liberia

Many Africans don't trust the health system. That complicates the response. (n.d.). Retrieved, March 9, 2021, from https://www.washingtonpost.com/politics/2020/02/18/coronavirus-is-about-hit-africa-here-are-big-challenges/

Mcdowell, R., & Donohoe. (2019, February 19). *What Is the Difference Between Book Value & Market Value Per Share of Common Stock?* https://finance.zacks.com/difference-between-book-value-market-value-per-share-common-stock-4533.html

Motambo, A. (2020, March 19). *Why few coronavirus cases in Africa came from China*. Retrieved, April 9, 2020, from https://www.nation.co.ke/news/africa/Why-few-coronavirus-cases-in-Africa-have-come-from-China/1066-5496368-ulwl32z/index.html

Mwaura, W. (2020, March 9). *Letter from Africa: The spread of coronavirus prejudice in Kenya*. Retrieved May 02, 2020, from https://www.bbc.com/news/world-africa-51770856

Patrick, A. (2020). *Rwanda's Kagame thanks Jack Ma for 'huge shot in the arm' after receiving a donation of test kits*. Retrieved, March 30, 2020, from https://www.cnn.com/2020/03/16/africa/jack-ma-donate-masks-coronavirus-africa/index.html

Patterson, A. (2020, February 18). *The coronavirus is about to hit Africa. Here are the big challenges. Many Africans don't trust the health system. That complicates the response*. Academic Press.

Patterson, A. (2020). *The coronavirus is about to hit Africa. Here are the big challenges*. Academic Press.

Penny, J. (2020, March 15). *African nations turn the tables, imposing travel restrictions against U.S., Europe, and China to stave off coronavirus*. Retrieved April 10 2020 from https://theintercept.com/2020/03/15/african-nations-turn-the-tables-imposing-travel-restrictions-against-u-s-europe-and-china-to-stave-off-coronavirus/

Ritchie, D. (n.d.). *Don't blame China for coronavirus, says Chinese ambassador to SA*. Retrieved March 30, 2020, from https://www.iol.co.za/weekend-argus/news/don't-blame-china-for-coronavirus-says-Chinese-ambassador-to-sa-44291500

United States Agency for International Development. (2020). https://openpayrolls.com/federal/united-states-agency-for-international-development#:~:text=The%20average%20employee%20salary%20for,higher%20than%20other%20federal%20agencies

Xia, H. (2018 August 21). *Chinese medical service contributes to the healthcare of African people*. http://www.xinhuanet.com/english/2018-08/21/c_137407868.htm

Chapter 8
The African Continent During and the Corona (COVID-19) Pandemic

ABSTRACT

There have been a lot of changes during this COVID-19 pandemic that will affect the relationship between PRC and the African continent. Some of these changes have been in the interpersonal relationship between ordinary Chinese and individuals of African descent. These changes have affected the diplomatic relationship and its effects on healthcare developmental projects. These projects have been affected by images on social media on how the Chinese mistreat Africans in China. Social media has been an important tool to affect the dynamic in these relationships. These social media outlets have been instrumental in the availability of mistreated Africans in the PRC. The United States of America, The People's Republic of China, and the African continent will be in a new era in a diplomatic relationship after the corona (COVID-19) pandemic. Whoever has the best game plan will win the hearts and minds of Africans.

DOI: 10.4018/978-1-7998-4450-1.ch008

Personal Opinion

***As a personal disclosure, I Leo Bachi Eyombo the author of the book was a Chinese Exchange Professor at Jinhua Professional Polytechnic University and lived in the (PRC) for (2012-2013).

I lived in China for two years and did not get any eye-opening racism moments except an occasion curious touch on my hair or face. Most Chinese people I meet were extremely very nice, helpful, and accommodating. My student was very accepting as the only faculty member that was of African descent. They were extremely academically curious about my background, life in America, and family. They were always common discussions on my Ivy league educational experience and my daily experience in China. Eventually, some of these conversations trickle down to Chinese Foreign Aid that initiates the idea of this book. Most Chinese individuals were aware of Chinese Foreign AID to developing countries but they were not conscious of the importance of healthcare aid. As mention in this early in this text that is an area that has grown in Africa from the early 1960s.

There has been a lot of changes in PRC healthcare during this COVID-19 pandemic that will affect the relationship between (PRC) and the African continent. Some of these changes have been in the interpersonal relationship between ordinary Chinese and peoples of African descent. Social media has been an important tool to affect the dynamic in these relationships. There have been several sites on social media platforms to show the struggles or mistreatment of Africans in China. With social media being the mode of most young people's news feeds, the images of the Chinese abusing Africans and evicting them from their homes have been a major hindrance in daily diplomacy between these two partners.

Chinese mistreatment of Africans for decades was not a major story due to the lack of information and limited social media accessibility. Most Africans did not have smartphone hence could not see the negative stereotype of Chinese in the media about Africans. The (PRC) has been maintaining an image of a win-win partnership with Africa. While Africans have accepted the Chinese in their closed communities and supporting these partnerships, the Chinese on their part have not been honest. As more African have gotten used to smartphone technology, this availability has been supported mostly by Chinese brands. These brands have been a major supplier of the African continent connectivity to the world, through these smartphones technology. Ironically, the images and/footages of Africans being mistreated in China by the Chinese have been brought to the limelight by the use of Chinese branded smartphones. These phone has also be used for healthcare digital records and technology.

The (PRC) understands the importance of healthy relationships in Africa and with Africans to maintain its superpower status in the global order. Chinese understands that China and its people are a great superpower to help the Africa continent and its peoples transform to the digital age. Thus Africa must be a part of the support structure to build and maintain Chinese greatness in the modern world. Africans are accepting the position to be self-determined and respected in the global community as equal partners. Africa has changed from the era of the cold war, independence, information technology, and a digital era. The continent has a young population that is extremely proactive and driven by the images that are shown on social media. The Corona pandemic has been a breaking point between Chinese and African diplomacy. These young Africans are in no mode to accommodate the mistakes of the independence generation of the 1950s to the digital era.

Leung (2020) the rise in reported discrimination comes after China's condemnation of racist attacks on ethnically Chinese people around the world as the coronavirus has spread. It also follows Beijing's attempts to stave off a second wave of infections after beating back the original outbreak, even reopening Wuhan, the city where the outbreak was first reported, on April 8, 2020. The majority of officially reported cases in China are now imported, mostly from Chinese nationals returning home after all foreign nationals were banned from entry in late March 2020. Mathews, (2020) an anthropology professor at the Chinese University of Hong Kong who has spent time with African communities in Guangzhou, says Africans in the city face discrimination on a day-to-day basis. These discrimination incidences are not encouraged by the Chinese government but show a disconnect with the local Chinese government. This major disconnect between the local Chinese government and the national government which includes the Chinese Foreign Services has been a problem during this pandemic.

The ability for these young Africans to see how others are treated has been the source of some of the major conflicts between Africans and the Chinese in the last couple of months. Also, the development of alternative media has been a contributing fact to some of these COVID-19 conflicts. Some of these shows like the Dr. Mumbi Show on YouTube have been a point for anti-Chinese sentiments in the African continent. These shows have shown a not so flattening side of the Chinese government, its citizens, and how they interact with average Africans. These reports on YouTube, as an alternative news channel are not evidence-based nor completely factual. They are extremely entertaining but lack the fair and balanced view of some traditional media.

Africans have been very suspicious of International organizations. For example, non-traditional media is very suspicious of the Gates Foundation. One African academician (Prof. PLO Lumumba) refers to the Gate foundation as "The Gates of HELL foundation". That the goals of the Gates Foundation are not the goals of Africa. Their strategy is the reduction of the African population via population control healthcare projects.

Traditional Media

I will like to make it clear that traditional media has never been fair in analyzing the African relationship with the Chinese nor the United States of America. Most traditional media reporting on African issues has been biased, to the African goals, agenda, and presentation. The traditional media has no interest in making some of these reports fair and balance. Among traditional media reporting on African relationships to the world, Al Jazeera seems to be the fairest from the African perspective. The void of a fair and balance traditional media source had led to alternative news media like YouTube, Twitter, Facebook, and some blog pages on the internet.

The alternative media (Non-traditional) has been the source of most of the social media news for China about the coronavirus pandemic, falsehood on treatment, and misinformation of Africans. This misinformation is even more important to the average African perspective of the world. The mistrust of the average African to traditional media has expanded a new way for information to be disseminated among the young from Alexandria, Egypt to Cape Town, South Africa. Most young Africans today are more aware of the world that they live in than their fathers and even individuals in the western world.

According to (Marsh, et al. 2020) on April 4 allegation that a Nigerian national with Covid-19 had attacked a Chinese nurse who tried to stop him from leaving an isolation ward at a Guangzhou Hospital is the start of all the conflict. The report was shared widely on social media, and local Africans spoke to CNN about the racist backlash against the African community. While the Chinese social media was lighting-up with this story, the version of the situation was completely different from the Social media accounts across the world. Then on April 7, Guangzhou authorities said five Nigerians had tested positive for Covid-19. The Guangzhou authorities upgrade the risk level, fearing a cluster among the African community, of Yuexiu and Baiyun in the city. During the COVID-19 crisis, International diplomacy and soft power have not been a priority in the containment.

The local government reported 111 imported cases of Covid-19 in Guangzhou, with 28 patients from the United Kingdom and 18 from the United States. In interviews with CNN, Americans and British nationals in Guangzhou said they had not heard reports of forced testing, home evictions, and additional quarantine measures being imposed on members of their communities (Marsh, 2020). But among individual of African descent, the eviction and forced detention was on the rise and had been shared among social media site all over the world.

African migrants were being evicted from their apartment and hotel rooms in the middle of the night and forced into quarantine in Guangzhou the third-largest city in China. These scenes went viral on social media causing widespread anger in Africa and have snowballed into an embarrassing and awkward diplomatic scandal for china (Zhou, 2020). Africans have responded very negatively towards some of these videos on social media, by attacking Chinese interest all across Africa. These might be the spare of the moment or just African trying to get the attention of their government to curve Chinese interests and annexation in their communities.

Zhou (2020) explains that Yu, a YouTuber made an explanation video on Chinese culture since 2018 claims that racism is a profoundly serious issue in China and singling out foreigners is a moral wrong. But why these perceived discrimination situations happen to have more to do with the Chinese system? It is a system that puts the growth of the GDP per head above the maltreatment of fellow humans. The explanation given by this alternative media source proclaimed these actions are done to motivate an increase in GDP and reduction of accidents.

African will beg to differ that they have seen pure signs of Chinese racism against people of African descent. African YouTubers claim that their government is not doing enough to respond to the racism from the picture and videos from the Chinese Southern city of Guangzhou. These pictures have invoked anger and resentment against the Chinese community leaving across the African continent. The young Africans believe their government is selling them out to the Chinese for pennies on a dollar. They in turn have had no choice but to take the laws into their hands and burn some Chinese factories in a place like Nigeria and Ghana.

The Chinese claim the rise of the new infections could mean going back to lockdown which will drag their economy and cause social instability. They say radical measures such as blocking roads, taping, and welding doors may have violated their people's property and personal privacy but had been a success in managing the COVID-19 pandemic. Hence this decision to quarantine Africans was a policy done without any racial prejudice. The decision to extend quarantine for most African shows that the Chinese Communist government has a disconnect between policymakers and local government officials.

People of African descent all over the world see racism in the actions of the Chinese government putting Africans out on the streets from their home and hotel rooms to reduce the COVID-19 cases as a malicious organized, coordinated effort to reduce the population of people of African descent in the city of Guangzhou. A video of a Nigerian Consular confronting the Guangzhou local official in April 2020 went viral on social media. In response, the Nigerian government summoned the Chinese Ambassador for some serious explanation on the behavior of Chinese police toward Nigeria citizens in China.

Sun (2020) acknowledged the implicit and discrimination against African, or more broadly, "black people" is not new and had been observed long before the COVID-19 crisis. While the Chinese government seeks a good relationship with Africa, the Chinese people are still overtly discriminative toward people of African descent in China. Beijing claims that all foreigners are treated equally but fails to acknowledge African migrants from developing countries might be financially stressed by mandatory quarantine costing about $40-$50 per day. The US state department sent a travel alert to the city of Guangzhou for Americans (Black Americans in particular) due to the African crisis.

Americans, on the other hand, have been absent during the COVID-19 pandemic in Africa, the degree of mistrust by African with echoes of a vaccine trial in Africa has increase conspiracy theories about western aid programs. The idea of the founder of The Gates Foundation (Bill Gates) making predictions of the destructions COVID-19 will cause across the Africa continent increased more conspiracy theories on social media and alternative news feed. The Bill and Melinda Gates Foundation has been a major supporter of most African health care projects. But so has the questions on their motives and intentions to provide these health care projects like population control.

According to Assistant Secretary of State for African Affairs Nagy (2020), the United States of America and the African partnership have continued to grow even stronger. We (American) are by far the largest donor nation to the African continent and our impact is felt across the board. The United States has committed more than $100 billion over the past 20 years towards public health on the continent and trained over 285,000 healthcare workers. During the Bush-era with President's Emergency Plan for AIDS Relief (PEPFAR) alone, over 18 million lives were saved in 18 years. These statistics look great, but why are Africans still in need of proper health care? The old USAID model of top-down aids has not been efficient nor progressive. Africans are still struggling to build a health care system to support their citizens. A new strategy for health care support needs to be individualized from a community need assessment approach.

The United States of America is actively working to save lives in Africa by fighting Malaria, Ebola, Avian Flu, and Cholera. The President's Malaria Initiative (PMI) has helped saved over 7 million lives while preventing over a billion cases of Malaria in the last 20 years. Where PMI is present, Malaria deaths have seen a 60 percent decline since 2006. Now, in the fight against COVID-19, that commitment continues. No other nation is doing more than we are (Nagy, 2020).

Yes, this statement is correct, but the problem is how these healthcare operations had been carried out. Contrary, the Chinese have been blamed for bringing manpower from China, the United States has developed an international development industry that depends on Africa's health care project. While the PMI has been effective in some areas and reduces preventable death the bigger benefactor has been the international development industry in Washington DC.

Of the more than $780 million the U.S. has pledged worldwide to fight the virus, close to $250 million is geared towards Africa. Our (America) response goes beyond this new money. In places such as Ghana, Senegal, Uganda, Sierra Leonne, and Mauritania, field hospitals, tents, and ambulances intended for international peace-keeping missions were repurposed for COVID-19 efforts. Our mutual trust built over the years has also played a role given the enormous efforts by African Governments, airlines, and others to help repatriate over 10,000 Americans from the continent (Nagy, 2020).

The United States had endless goodwill during the cold war but the idea of trust has been reduced due to the failure of some of these programs to be maintained long-term. A new president (government) in the United State means a new priority in international development. The failure of the United States to take leadership in the pandemic has left a void in the international developing world. Americans still flirting with the policy of making American great again but here is an opportunity to keep America great.

Furthermore, it is not just our government leading; we also have what we call an "all-of-America" approach; Businesses, NGOs, faith-based organizations have contributed. Together, Americans have committed nearly $6.5 billion, including the experts whom we have deployed worldwide and those still conducting tutorials via video conference today, and the doctors and the public health professionals who have been trained thanks to U.S. money and educational institutions (Nagy, 2020). After all these expectations on American ground games, we are still missing a great opportunity to build trust and to keep America great.

An agreement between UNICEF, the Bauchi State Education Board (Nigeria), state radio and television boards, and local universities, USAID has supported the COVID-19 contingency plan for the state's education sector to help ensure a continuum of teaching and learning while children quarantine at home (Global Health Alert 4, 2020). Here is some private-public partnership collaboration that has been beneficial to Nigerian students. These projects should be enhanced and encourage for a better outcome for the average African. Most of these students will remember the greatness of American when they become young adults.

International Institutions

Although the United States approach has been to give the autonomy to the state to decide on how to manage the resources while having a hand-free policy in Africa. These hands-free policies have led to some alternative media to dump the USA the "Divided States" for having such divisive policies for African countries. So, while Americans are looking for the State of New York for COVID-19 leadership. The international leadership void for COVID-19 has led other international institutions like the World Bank and International Monetary Fund more active to support COVID-19 operations in Africa.

What should the relationship be for Africa after COVID-19 a SWOT Analysis?

Strength

Africans should use the COVID-19 pandemic to develop a better health care system. The united in strength ideals of a United African States should be the foundation for a single-payer health care insurance system in Africa. In Nigeria for example, most of the rich seek treatment overseas, so the COVID-19 pandemic has been a test for the need for a better health care system.

Weakness: The African relationship with other international donor countries. The relationship between the United State of American and the PRC is unreliable. Therefore, Africa needs to rely more on Africa. There has to be a collaborative effort to come together in healthcare to build an efficient healthcare system. Africa should seek African solutions. The lack of universal African standards for health, pharmaceutical, food, and visa entry has been a major handicap in the crisis management of this pandemic. Uniformity should be a long-term goal for the African continent to get better representation, of all people of African descent in the world.

Africa needs to be a place of complete and total independence financially, socio-economically, and politically. There should be a balance of power between the leaders and their citizens. People need to understand that the people are the real power behind the government, not the selfish and self-centered leadership that agrees to unimaginable long-term deals with economic resources of the western world and China.

The brain drain of African intellectuals due to a lack of civil discourse and academic independence is a major problem. The separation of the academic, legal, and health care sectors should be universal across Africa. These institutions should be managed by a local board appointed by the regional government not the central government. An increase in the exchange of ideas will be the building blocks to maintain operations and develop new health care strategies for Africa.

Opportunities

Africans should develop a program for returning scientists, educators, and health care providers and experts. There should also be a seed fund for new business development and innovation for a new university graduate to be an entrepreneur. These small loans should not exceed eight thousand ($8000), issued in four (4) installments. This will be Africa's opportunity to start developing small manufacturing industries. The true building block for a developing economy is the small business support system. This will help the average African in gaining employment and develop a small business industry to support the economy long term. These programs should be processed and impact evaluated to achieve program efficiency.

According to Pettinger (2018), the law of diminishing returns states a decline in productivity improvements from a fixed capital. When you have very low productivity in agriculture like in most African countries, a small investment (e.g. motorized tractor) can give a high rate of return and significantly increase output. One advantage that poorer countries in African can replicate existing technology and working practices developed by advanced economies. For example, in Africa, many citizens never had a landline or fax machine but jumped straight to the mobile phone and the internet has benefited from very cheap phone calls. This new technology has significantly improved communication in developing economies and skipped out levels of developmental investment. African should also focus on biotechnology and nanotechnology to lead these areas as their flagship industry.

Africa needs to use this COVID-19 period to evaluate its relationship with the (PRC) and the United States of America. The fundamentals of their relationship can be readdressed through bilateral negotiations using the Africa Union (AU). The AU should be used not as an international organization but as collective bargaining media to look out for the average African interest. The (AU) should draft a simple document to guide most of its members to institution business visas, education collaboration, and innovation for new business and entrepreneurship. It's about time the (AU) parliament become a real tool for African good governance.

Focus Industries

Africa needs to focus on four different industries post-COVID-19 to take control of its developmental destiny. These industries are Agricultural, Mining, management of economic resources, and Healthcare.

Agriculture Industry: The African continent has been a dumping ground for USAID excess American milk, rice, and oil. The Chinese have found a market of no limit on local provisions. So, there are Chinese farms all across Africa with support from the PRC while the African farmer cannot compete. The local government should take complete control of the agricultural section with a small business innovation support strategy to build commercial farming. Governments should target young African graduates from top African institutions to get into farming. There is nothing like fair trade if African governments cannot support their citizens to farm, like the PRC or the Unites States of America. The basic tomatoes market in Africa should be supported for economic advantage. They can be a division of labor strategy among (AU) nations to evaluation the best local environment for the farming industries.

Mining Industry

ALL mines must be licensed and managed by the local board in conjunction with local governments. Foreigners regardless of finance should be ban from investing in the mining industry. The development of Partnerships with foreign entities has failed Africa and a source of corruption. There is no good model except for the Botswana model. The Botswana diamond model may be replicated in an industry where there is strong internal governance. The idea of a rogue individual running a small, illegal, environment-hazardous mine should be put to an end. The small-scale Chinese miners should be shot down and fifty percent of all mine revenues not profits should be invested in the local municipal.

HEALTHCARE

Threat

There are major threats that will affect (PRC) and the United States. These threats are economically, socially, and diplomatic. The economic threat will be a major reduction of trade between (PRC) and Africa. The United States has been absent through the COVID-19 pandemic because they are dealing with the worst economic decline since the great depression. The Chinese on the other hand, have been much affected by the social media stories of their discrimination and racism against Africans in China. A great backlash against Chinese migrants in Africa will decrease the economic and social advantages on the ground. The disruption of the Chinese ground game might lead to an increase in durable goods and a decrease in Chinese traveling to Africa.

As the (AU) becomes more active in this decision-making on the African continent, the position of the individual states will be a threat. These might result in a lot of Ballot revolution (BR) across the continent. Ballot Revolution will be defined as a transition state or where young people become more involved and take over the local or central government. Contrary, to the CIA report in the 1970s, earlier mentioned, younger African are becoming more involved because they can see the effects of bad governance on their daily lives. (BR) is a major threat to business as usual in Africa and a major opportunity for change in Africa.

Leontief (1973, Pettinger 2018) acknowledged the catch-up effect (or convergence theory) suggests that poorer countries will experience a higher rate of economic growth and, over time, get closer to the income levels of the developed world. Africans should try to make this a reality, by really investing in the private section and collaborating with fellow Africans. They should be some protective measure to encourage the local African in developing their economy after the COVID-19 pandemic.

REFERENCES

Global Health Alert. (2020). *U.S. Mission Nigeria.* https://ng.usembassy.gov/usaid-helps-keep-bauchi-students-learning-under-lockdown-through-e-learning-collaboration/

Leontif, W. (1966). *Essays in Economics: Theories and Theorizing.* Oxford University Press.

Leung, H. (2020). *African in Guangzhou say they are targets of discrimination.* Retrieved, March 12, 2021, from https://time.com/5820389/africans-guangzhou-china-coronavirus-discrimination/

Marsh, J., Deng, S., & Gan, N. (2020). *Africans in Guangzhou are on edge after many are left homeless amid rising xenophobia as China fights the second wave of coronavirus.* Retrieved, April 04, 2020, from https://www.cnn.com/2020/04/10/china/africans-guangzhou-china-coronavirus-hnk-intl/index.html

Mash, J. (2020, April 13). *Beijing faces a diplomatic crisis after reports of mistreatment of African in China.* Retrieved, April 24, 2020, from https://www.cnn.com/2020/04/13/asia/china-guangzhou-african-blacklash-hnk-intl/index.html

Matthew, G. (2020). *Will China Ever Have a black President?* Retrieved from, March 13, 2021https://www.sixthtone.com/news/1001975/will-china-ever-have-a-black-president%3F

Nagy, T. (2020). *Press Briefing on COVID-19 in Africa and the US. Response with Ambassador Tibor P. Nagy Assistant Secretary, Bureau of Africa Affairs*. https://ng.usembassy.gov/telephonic-press-briefing-on-covid-19-in-africa-and-the-u-s-response-with-ambassador-tibor-p-nagy-assistant-secretary-bureau-of-african-affairs/

Pettinger, T. (2018). *The Catch-Up Effect*. Retrieved March 23, 2020, from https://www.economicshelp.org/blog/143243/economics/the-catch-up-effect/

Sun, Y. (2020). *COVID-19, Africans' hardships in China, and the future of Africa-China relations*. https://www.brookings.edu/blog/africa-in-focus/2020/04/17/covid-19-africans-hardships-in-china-and-the-future-of-africa-china-relations/

Zhou, Y. (2020). *A Chinese YouTuber shows how China's political system ends up with Africans being mistreated*. Retrieved March 13, 2021, from https://qz.com/africa/1843572/how-chinas-political-system-has-africans-being-mistreated/amp/

Related Readings

To continue IGI Global's long-standing tradition of advancing innovation through emerging research, please find below a compiled list of recommended IGI Global book chapters and journal articles in the areas of issues such as racism in PRC residing in Africa and the USA's struggle with coronavirus. These related readings will provide additional information and guidance to further enrich your knowledge and assist you with your own research.

Adjin-Tettey, T. D. (2020). Healthcare Gets Smarter. In S. Umair (Ed.), *Mobile Devices and Smart Gadgets in Medical Sciences* (pp. 39–55). IGI Global. doi:10.4018/978-1-7998-2521-0.ch003

Al Balkhi, A. (2019). The Healthcare Strategic Practice in Abu Dhabi, United Arab Emirates. In F. Albadri & Y. A. Nasereddin (Eds.), *Strategic Thinking, Planning, and Management Practice in the Arab World* (pp. 75–91). IGI Global. doi:10.4018/978-1-5225-8048-5.ch004

Altinpulluk, H. (2018). A Systematic Review of Mobile Health in Education From 2000 to 2016. *International Journal of Reliable and Quality E-Healthcare*, *7*(3), 1–17. doi:10.4018/IJRQEH.2018070101

Andriopoulou, F., Birkos, K., & Lymberopoulos, D. (2017). A Novel Hierarchical Group-Based Overlay Healthcare Network. *International Journal of E-Health and Medical Communications*, *8*(4), 81–102. doi:10.4018/IJEHMC.2017100105

Badru, F. A. (2019). The Nexus of Tamed Bureaucracy and Better Health Outcomes for Consumers in Nigeria's Health Institutions. In A. N. Eneanya (Ed.), *Human Rights, Public Values, and Leadership in Healthcare Policy* (pp. 48–64). IGI Global. doi:10.4018/978-1-5225-6133-0.ch003

Bareach, H. Y., Malik, W., Sohail, R., Javaid, A., & Jalil, M. N. (2019). Hierarchical Planning Models for Public Healthcare Supply Chains. In A. Taghipour (Ed.), *Hierarchical Planning and Information Sharing Techniques in Supply Chain Management* (pp. 86–122). IGI Global. doi:10.4018/978-1-5225-7299-2.ch003

Beeman, T. E., & Dean, G. M. (2019). Developing Healthcare Leaders for the Future. In V. A. Storey & T. E. Beeman (Eds.), *Preparing Physicians to Lead in the 21st Century* (pp. 26–35). IGI Global. doi:10.4018/978-1-5225-7576-4.ch002

Bobrowicz-Campos, E., & Matos, A. P. (2020). Ageing and Health in the Digital Society. In D. Mendes, C. Fonseca, M. J. Lopes, J. García-Alonso, & J. M. Murillo (Eds.), *Exploring the Role of ICTs in Healthy Aging* (pp. 34–55). IGI Global. doi:10.4018/978-1-7998-1937-0.ch003

Bouchard, B., Bouchard, K., Gaboury, S., & Bouzouane, A. (2018). Smart Senior Residences. In B. K. Mishra & R. Kumar (Eds.), *Big Data Management and the Internet of Things for Improved Health Systems* (pp. 65–85). IGI Global. doi:10.4018/978-1-5225-5222-2.ch005

Candereli, Z. O., Burmaoglu, S., Kidak, L. B., & Gungor, D. O. (2020). Applying Blockchain Technologies in Healthcare. In Y. Demir Uslu, H. Dinçer, & S. Yüksel (Eds.), *Multidimensional Perspectives and Global Analysis of Universal Health Coverage* (pp. 69–92). IGI Global. doi:10.4018/978-1-7998-2329-2.ch003

Chakraborty, S., & Bhatt, V. (2020). Interactional Resource Adoption. In L. Gaur, A. Solanki, V. Jain, & D. Khazanchi (Eds.), *Handbook of Research on Engineering Innovations and Technology Management in Organizations* (pp. 253–268). IGI Global. doi:10.4018/978-1-7998-2772-6.ch014

Clack, L. (2021). Examination of Quality of Life in Workplace Environments. In Encyclopedia of Organizational Knowledge, Administration, and Technology (pp. 2638-2650). IGI Global. http://doi:10.4018/978-1-7998-3473-1.ch182

Clack, L., & Nagi, B. (2020). Examination of the Impact of Patient Engagement Tools on Patient Satisfaction. *International Journal of Patient-Centered Healthcare, 10*(1), 37–46. doi:10.4018/IJPCH.2020010103

Costanza, F. (2018). Governing Patients' Mobility to Pursue Public Value. In G. M. Azevedo, J. da Silva Oliveira, R. P. Marques, & A. D. Ferreira (Eds.), *Handbook of Research on Modernization and Accountability in Public Sector Management* (pp. 276–299). IGI Global. doi:10.4018/978-1-5225-3731-1.ch013

Costanza, F. (2020). Effects of Patient Mobility on Healthcare Systems. In G. Azevedo, J. Oliveira, R. Marques, & A. Ferreira (Eds.), *Tools, Strategies, and Practices for Modern and Accountable Public Sector Management* (pp. 227–257). IGI Global. doi:10.4018/978-1-7998-1385-9.ch009

Dadgar, M., & Joshi, K. D. (2020). Ethically Building Business Intelligence in Healthcare. In J. Khuntia, X. Ning, & M. Tanniru (Eds.), *Theory and Practice of Business Intelligence in Healthcare* (pp. 256–278). IGI Global. doi:10.4018/978-1-7998-2310-0.ch012

Dawkes, S., & Cheung, S. T. (2018). United Kingdom Health Promotion Initiatives for Healthy Aging. In B. Fong, A. Ng, & P. Yuen (Eds.), *Sustainable Health and Long-Term Care Solutions for an Aging Population* (pp. 91–102). IGI Global. doi:10.4018/978-1-5225-2633-9.ch005

DelConte, A., & Gast, M. J. (2019). Design and Program Elements of a Clinical Leadership Program. In V. A. Storey & T. E. Beeman (Eds.), *Preparing Physicians to Lead in the 21st Century* (pp. 94–114). IGI Global. doi:10.4018/978-1-5225-7576-4.ch006

Demirel, E. T., & Emul, E. (2020). Evaluation of the Broken Windows Theory in Terms of Patient Safety. In Y. Demir Uslu, H. Dinçer, & S. Yüksel (Eds.), *Multidimensional Perspectives and Global Analysis of Universal Health Coverage* (pp. 266–284). IGI Global. doi:10.4018/978-1-7998-2329-2.ch010

Duncan, T., Hanney, G. J., Burrell, D. N., & Rahim, E. (2020). Effective Integration of Technology and Human Capital Development in Healthcare. In S. O. Atiku (Ed.), *Human Capital Formation for the Fourth Industrial Revolution* (pp. 268–285). IGI Global. doi:10.4018/978-1-5225-9810-7.ch011

Edirippulige, S., & Senanayake, B. (2020). Professional Practices for Digital Healthcare. In K. Sandhu (Ed.), *Opportunities and Challenges in Digital Healthcare Innovation* (pp. 97–112). IGI Global. doi:10.4018/978-1-7998-3274-4.ch006

Edoh, T. O. (2019). Internet-of-Things-Enabled Pre-Screening for Diseases. In T. Edoh, P. Pawar, & S. Mohammad (Eds.), *Pre-Screening Systems for Early Disease Prediction, Detection, and Prevention* (pp. 1–49). IGI Global. doi:10.4018/978-1-5225-7131-5.ch001

Edu, S. A., & Agozie, D. Q. (2020). Exploring Factors Influencing Big Data and Analytics Adoption in Healthcare Management. In R. Boateng (Ed.), *Handbook of Research on Managing Information Systems in Developing Economies* (pp. 413–428). IGI Global. doi:10.4018/978-1-7998-2610-1.ch020

Elgujja, A. A. (2020). Impact of Information Technology on Patient Confidentiality Rights. In R. W. McHaney, I. Reychev, J. Azuri, M. E. McHaney, & R. Moshonov (Eds.), *Impacts of Information Technology on Patient Care and Empowerment* (pp. 365–387). IGI Global. doi:10.4018/978-1-7998-0047-7.ch018

Eneanya, A. N. (2019). Integrating Human Rights, Equity, and Social Justice in Health Policies in America and Nigeria. In A. N. Eneanya (Ed.), *Human Rights, Public Values, and Leadership in Healthcare Policy* (pp. 179–202). IGI Global. doi:10.4018/978-1-5225-6133-0.ch009

Eneanya, A. N. (2019). Linking Primary Healthcare Policies With Health System for Improved Health Outcomes in Nigeria. In A. N. Eneanya (Ed.), *Human Rights, Public Values, and Leadership in Healthcare Policy* (pp. 87–114). IGI Global. doi:10.4018/978-1-5225-6133-0.ch005

Esmaeilzadeh, P. (2018). Challenges and Opportunities of Health Information Exchange (HIE) From Health Consumers' Perspective. *International Journal of E-Health and Medical Communications, 9*(3), 20–42. doi:10.4018/IJEHMC.2018070102

Esteves, M., Esteves, M., & Abelha, A. C. (2020). A New System to Assist Elders' Self-Care and Their Informal Caregivers. *International Journal of Reliable and Quality E-Healthcare, 9*(1), 50–65. doi:10.4018/IJRQEH.2020010105

Faruk, N., Surajudeen-Bakinde, N., Abdulkarim, A., Oloyede, A. A., Olawoyin, L., Bello, O. W., Popoola, S. I., & Edoh, T. O. (2020). Rural Healthcare Delivery in Sub-Saharan Africa. *International Journal of Healthcare Information Systems and Informatics*, *15*(3), 1–21. doi:10.4018/IJHISI.2020070101

Fowowe, M. A., & Arogundade, K. K. (2021). Impact of Employees' Empowerment on Perceived Quality of Service Delivery in the Tertiary Health Institutions. In Encyclopedia of Organizational Knowledge, Administration, and Technology (pp. 2014-2030). IGI Global. http://doi:10.4018/978-1-7998-3473-1.ch138

Fredrickson, J. (2020). Billing and Review Perspectives in Healthcare. In J. Khuntia, X. Ning, & M. Tanniru (Eds.), *Theory and Practice of Business Intelligence in Healthcare* (pp. 18–67). IGI Global. doi:10.4018/978-1-7998-2310-0.ch002

Galli, B. J., Kaviani, M. A., Bottani, E., & Murino, T. (2017). Shared Leadership and Key Innovation Indicators in Six Sigma Projects. *International Journal of Strategic Decision Sciences*, *8*(4), 1–45. doi:10.4018/IJSDS.2017100101

Galli, B. J., Kaviani, M. A., Bottani, E., & Murino, T. (2019). An Investigation of the Development of Shared Leadership on the Six Sigma Project Life Cycle. *International Journal of Information Technology Project Management*, *10*(4), 15–78. doi:10.4018/IJITPM.2019100102

Greer, A., Selladurai, R. I., Pfeifle, A. L., Selladurai, R., & Hobson, C. J. (2020). Effective Teamwork and Healthcare Delivery Outcomes. In Evaluating Challenges and Opportunities for Healthcare Reform (pp. 77-99). IGI Global. doi:10.4018/978-1-7998-2949-2.ch004

Hung, W., Chang, L., & Lee, M. (2017). Success of National Healthcare Services Information Systems. In Handbook of Research on Technology Adoption, Social Policy, and Global Integration (pp. 328-354). IGI Global. doi:10.4018/978-1-5225-2668-1.ch016

Idowu, D., & King, G. (2018). Health Literacy and Ethnic Minority Populations. In V. E. Papalois & M. Theodosopoulou (Eds.), *Optimizing Health Literacy for Improved Clinical Practices* (pp. 210–227). IGI Global. doi:10.4018/978-1-5225-4074-8.ch012

Ighodalo, A. (2019). Policy Value and Primary Healthcare Delivery in Rural Nigeria. In A. N. Eneanya (Ed.), *Human Rights, Public Values, and Leadership in Healthcare Policy* (pp. 116–132). IGI Global. doi:10.4018/978-1-5225-6133-0.ch006

Ilie, V., & Sneha, S. (2018). A Three Country Study for Understanding Physicians' Engagement With Electronic Information Resources Pre and Post System Implementation. *Journal of Global Information Management, 26*(2), 48–73. doi:10.4018/JGIM.2018040103

Iyamu, T. (2020). Examining E-Government Enabling of E-Health Service Through the Lens of Structuration Theory. *International Journal of Sociotechnology and Knowledge Development, 12*(3), 26–40. doi:10.4018/IJSKD.2020070102

Iyamu, T., & Shaanika, I. (2020). Factors Influencing the Use of Mobile Systems to Access Healthcare Big Data in a Namibian Public Hospital. *Information Resources Management Journal, 33*(3), 81–99. doi:10.4018/IRMJ.2020070104

Iyawa, G. E., Herselman, M., & Botha, A. (2019). Digital Health Innovation Ecosystems. *International Journal of Reliable and Quality E-Healthcare, 8*(2), 1–14. doi:10.4018/IJRQEH.2019040101

Iyawa, G. E., Langan-Martin, J., Sevalie, S., & Masikara, W. (2020). mHealth as Tools for Development in Mental Health. In Impacts of Information Technology on Patient Care and Empowerment (pp. 58-80). IGI Global. http://doi:10.4018/978-1-7998-0047-7.ch004

Kalina, J. (2019). Mental Health Clinical Decision Support Exploiting Big Data. In K. Chui & M. D. Lytras (Eds.), *Computational Methods and Algorithms for Medicine and Optimized Clinical Practice* (pp. 160–184). IGI Global. doi:10.4018/978-1-5225-8244-1.ch008

Karadayi-Usta, S., & Serdarasan, S. (2020). A Collaborative Framework for Medical Tourism Service Supply Chain Operations. In S. Paul & S. Kulshreshtha (Eds.), *Global Developments in Healthcare and Medical Tourism* (pp. 188–219). IGI Global. doi:10.4018/978-1-5225-9787-2.ch011

Katehakis, D. G., & Kouroubali, A. (2020). Digital Transformation Challenges for the Implementation of Quality Electronic Medical Records. In A. S. Moumtzoglou (Ed.), *Quality Assurance in the Era of Individualized Medicine* (pp. 63–91). IGI Global. doi:10.4018/978-1-7998-2390-2.ch003

Knepper, H. (2018). Healthcare in the United States. In H. Levine & K. Moreno (Eds.), *Positioning Markets and Governments in Public Management* (pp. 73–85). IGI Global. doi:10.4018/978-1-5225-4177-6.ch007

Koumpouros, Y., & Georgoulas, A. (2019). The Rise of mHealth Research in Europe. In A. Moumtzoglou (Ed.), *Mobile Health Applications for Quality Healthcare Delivery* (pp. 1–29). IGI Global. doi:10.4018/978-1-5225-8021-8.ch001

Latif, S., Khan, M. Y., Qayyum, A., Qadir, J., Usman, M., Ali, S. M., Abbasi, Q. H., & Imran, M. A. (2018). Mobile Technologies for Managing Non-Communicable Diseases in Developing Countries. In S. Paiva (Ed.), *Mobile Applications and Solutions for Social Inclusion* (pp. 261–287). IGI Global. doi:10.4018/978-1-5225-5270-3.ch011

Lemos, C. (2019). Innovation in Laboratory Medicine. In Handbook of Research on Business Models in Modern Competitive Scenarios (pp. 117-137). IGI Global. doi:10.4018/978-1-5225-7265-7.ch007

Liu, K. Y., Wong, B. H., Chu, M., & Leung, W. Y. (2018). The Continuum of Care. In B. Fong, A. Ng, & P. Yuen (Eds.), *Sustainable Health and Long-Term Care Solutions for an Aging Population* (pp. 71–90). IGI Global. doi:10.4018/978-1-5225-2633-9.ch004

Makovhololo, P., & Iyamu, T. (2020). A Framework to Guide ICT Solution for Language Barrier in South African Healthcare. *Journal of Cases on Information Technology*, *22*(2), 1–17. doi:10.4018/JCIT.2020040101

Malanga, D. F., & Chigona, W. (2018). Mobile Health Initiatives in Malawi. *International Journal of Privacy and Health Information Management*, *6*(1), 49–60. doi:10.4018/IJPHIM.2018010104

Marutha, N. S. (2020). Cooperative Collaboration Amongst Healthcare Institutions Towards Central Access to Medical with Patients Records. In C. T. Chisita (Ed.), *Cooperation and Collaboration Initiatives for Libraries and Related Institutions* (pp. 62–79). IGI Global. doi:10.4018/978-1-7998-0043-9.ch004

Masri, F., & Abdelrahman, M. (2019). An Explorative Study of Knowledge-Transfer Mechanism. In Y. A. Albastaki, A. I. Al-Alawi, & S. Abdulrahman Al-Bassam (Eds.), *Handbook of Research on Implementing Knowledge Management Strategy in the Public Sector* (pp. 18–54). IGI Global. doi:10.4018/978-1-5225-9639-4.ch002

Medhekar, A., & Haq, F. (2018). Urbanization and New Jobs Creation in Healthcare Services in India. In U. Benna & I. Benna (Eds.), *Urbanization and Its Impact on Socio-Economic Growth in Developing Regions* (pp. 198–218). IGI Global. doi:10.4018/978-1-5225-2659-9.ch010

Medhekar, A., & Nguyen, J. (2020). My Digital Healthcare Record. In K. Sandhu (Ed.), *Opportunities and Challenges in Digital Healthcare Innovation* (pp. 131–150). IGI Global. doi:10.4018/978-1-7998-3274-4.ch008

Melo, A. I., Santinha, G., & Lima, R. (2018). Measuring the Quality of Health Services Using SERVQUAL. In G. M. Azevedo, J. da Silva Oliveira, R. P. Marques, & A. D. Ferreira (Eds.), *Handbook of Research on Modernization and Accountability in Public Sector Management* (pp. 300–318). IGI Global. doi:10.4018/978-1-5225-3731-1.ch014

Moumtzoglou, A. S. (2019). The Nexus of M-Health and Self-Care. In A. Moumtzoglou (Ed.), *Mobile Health Applications for Quality Healthcare Delivery* (pp. 235–259). IGI Global. doi:10.4018/978-1-5225-8021-8.ch011

Mutingi, M. (2018). Towards a Customer-Centric Framework for Evaluation of E-Health Service Quality. In N. Gwangwava & M. Mutingi (Eds.), *E-Manufacturing and E-Service Strategies in Contemporary Organizations* (pp. 199–218). IGI Global. doi:10.4018/978-1-5225-3628-4.ch008

Nair, P. (2019). The Emerging Concept of an Inclusive mHealth Ecosystem in India. In C. Albuquerque (Ed.), *Emerging Trends and Innovations in Privacy and Health Information Management* (pp. 116–141). IGI Global. doi:10.4018/978-1-5225-8470-4.ch005

Ochonogor, W. C., & Mutula, S. M. (2020). The Use of Social Media by Medical Librarians for Inclusive Engagement in the Management of HIV/AIDS in Nigeria University Teaching Hospitals. In A. Tella (Ed.), *Handbook of Research on Digital Devices for Inclusivity and Engagement in Libraries* (pp. 1–24). IGI Global. doi:10.4018/978-1-5225-9034-7.ch001

Odeyinka, O. J., Ajibola, O. A., & Ndinechi, M. C. (2020). The Role and Trend of Information and Communications Technology Towards a Pervasive Healthcare System. *International Journal of Information Communication Technologies and Human Development, 12*(3), 59–73. doi:10.4018/IJICTHD.20200701.oa1

Price, R., & Shinn, S. (2020). A Strategic Overview and Vision of Simulation-Based Education in Healthcare in England. In Y. Qian (Ed.), *Teaching, Learning, and Leading With Computer Simulations* (pp. 1–36). IGI Global. doi:10.4018/978-1-7998-0004-0.ch001

Ramakrishnan, T., Kathuria, A., & Saldanha, T. J. (2020). Business Intelligence and Analytics (BI&A) Capabilities in Healthcare. In J. Khuntia, X. Ning, & M. Tanniru (Eds.), *Theory and Practice of Business Intelligence in Healthcare* (pp. 1–17). IGI Global. doi:10.4018/978-1-7998-2310-0.ch001

Rathi, M., & Pareek, V. (2019). Mobile Based Healthcare Tool an Integrated Disease Prediction & Recommendation System. *International Journal of Knowledge and Systems Science*, *10*(1), 38–62. doi:10.4018/IJKSS.2019010103

Riha, C. D. (2019). Tools and Considerations to Develop the Blueprint for the Next Generation of Clinical Care Technology. *International Journal of Biomedical and Clinical Engineering*, *8*(1), 1–8. doi:10.4018/IJBCE.2019010101

Rouzbehani, K. R., & Araghi, M. (2020). From Resource to Outcome. In N. Wickramasinghe (Ed.), *Handbook of Research on Optimizing Healthcare Management Techniques* (pp. 154–166). IGI Global. doi:10.4018/978-1-7998-1371-2.ch010

Saha, A., & Agarwal, N. (2018). *Social Support Assessment*. IGI Global. doi:10.4018/978-1-5225-4020-5.ch003

Saoud, M. S., Boubetra, A., & Attia, S. (2018). A Simulation Decision Support System for the Healthcare Emergency Department Optimization. In J. Tan (Ed.), *Handbook of Research on Emerging Perspectives on Healthcare Information Systems and Informatics* (pp. 347–367). IGI Global. doi:10.4018/978-1-5225-5460-8.ch015

Saripalle, R. K. (2019). Fast Health Interoperability Resources (FHIR). *International Journal of E-Health and Medical Communications*, *10*(1), 76–93. doi:10.4018/IJEHMC.2019010105

Sarkar, B. K. (2017). Big Data and Healthcare Data. *International Journal of Knowledge-Based Organizations*, *7*(4), 50–77. doi:10.4018/IJKBO.2017100104

Selladurai, R., & Selladurai, R. I. (2020). An Enhanced Healthcare Delivery System Model for the US. In Evaluating Challenges and Opportunities for Healthcare Reform (pp. 1-20). IGI Global. doi:10.4018/978-1-7998-2949-2.ch001

Selladurai, R., Selladurai, R. I., & VandeWerken, G. (2020). Exploring Innovative, Alternative Healthcare Models in the US. In Evaluating Challenges and Opportunities for Healthcare Reform (pp. 21-42). IGI Global. http://doi:10.4018/978-1-7998-2949-2.ch002

Senanayake, B., Tyagi, N., Zhou, X., & Edirippulige, S. (2020). Workforce Readiness and Digital Health Integration. In K. Sandhu (Ed.), *Opportunities and Challenges in Digital Healthcare Innovation* (pp. 170–185). IGI Global. doi:10.4018/978-1-7998-3274-4.ch010

Singhal, S., Jain, S., Rathi, M., & Sinha, A. (2019). Smart Technologies to Build Healthcare Models for Vision Impairment. In C. Chakraborty (Ed.), *Advanced Classification Techniques for Healthcare Analysis* (pp. 259–285). IGI Global. doi:10.4018/978-1-5225-7796-6.ch012

Smith, A. D. (2019). RFID Applications in Healthcare Systems From an Operational Perspective. *International Journal of Systems and Society*, *6*(2), 1–28. doi:10.4018/IJSS.2019070101

Sood, T. (2017). Services Marketing. In T. Sood (Ed.), *Strategic Marketing Management and Tactics in the Service Industry* (pp. 15–42). IGI Global. doi:10.4018/978-1-5225-2475-5.ch002

Storey, V. A. (2019). Developing Clinical Leaders. In V. A. Storey & T. E. Beeman (Eds.), *Preparing Physicians to Lead in the 21st Century* (pp. 71–92). IGI Global. doi:10.4018/978-1-5225-7576-4.ch005

Strydom, M. J., & Buckley, S. B. (2020). Big Data Intelligence and Perspectives in Darwinian Disruption. In M. Strydom & S. Buckley (Eds.), *AI and Big Data's Potential for Disruptive Innovation* (pp. 1–43). IGI Global. doi:10.4018/978-1-5225-9687-5.ch001

Sukkird, V., & Shirahada, K. (2018). E-Health Service Model for Asian Developing Countries. In Optimizing Current Practices in E-Services and Mobile Applications (pp. 214-232). IGI Global. http://doi:10.4018/978-1-5225-5026-6.ch011

Suomi, R., & Damalie, E. (2020). Public Reporting on Health and Social Care Services. In N. Wickramasinghe (Ed.), *Handbook of Research on Optimizing Healthcare Management Techniques* (pp. 33–53). IGI Global. doi:10.4018/978-1-7998-1371-2.ch003

Tiselius, E., Hägglund, E., & Pergert, P. (2020). Distressful Situations, Non-Supportive Work Climate, Threats to Professional and Private Integrity. In I. Souza & E. E. Fragkou (Eds.), *Handbook of Research on Medical Interpreting* (pp. 54–79). IGI Global. doi:10.4018/978-1-5225-9308-9.ch003

Turcu, C. E., & Turcu, C. O. (2018). New Perspectives on Sustainable Healthcare Delivery Through Web of Things. In A. Elçi (Ed.), *Handbook of Research on Contemporary Perspectives on Web-Based Systems* (pp. 166–187). IGI Global. doi:10.4018/978-1-5225-5384-7.ch009

Waldron, T. W., & DiAngelo, J. (2019). The Cohort Model. In V. A. Storey & T. E. Beeman (Eds.), *Preparing Physicians to Lead in the 21st Century* (pp. 36–55). IGI Global. doi:10.4018/978-1-5225-7576-4.ch003

Wang, C. (2019). The Strengths, Weaknesses, Opportunities, and Threats Analysis of Big Data Analytics in Healthcare. *International Journal of Big Data and Analytics in Healthcare*, *4*(1), 1–14. doi:10.4018/IJBDAH.2019010101

Wickramasinghe, N. (2020). Predictive Analytics to Support Clinical Decision Making. In N. Wickramasinghe (Ed.), *Handbook of Research on Optimizing Healthcare Management Techniques* (pp. 271–281). IGI Global. doi:10.4018/978-1-7998-1371-2.ch020

Wickramasinghe, N. (2020). The Need for Developing Learning Healthcare Organisations. In N. Wickramasinghe (Ed.), *Handbook of Research on Optimizing Healthcare Management Techniques* (pp. 1–15). IGI Global. doi:10.4018/978-1-7998-1371-2.ch001

Wickramasinghe, N., & Goldberg, S. (2020). Supporting a Value-Based Healthcare Paradigm With Digital Health and Wellness Personalised Monitoring Solutions. In K. Sandhu (Ed.), *Opportunities and Challenges in Digital Healthcare Innovation* (pp. 57–71). IGI Global. doi:10.4018/978-1-7998-3274-4.ch004

Yucesan, M., Mete, S., Gul, M., & Celik, E. (2020). A Fuzzy Decision-Making Model for the Key Performance Indicators of Hospital Service Quality Evaluation. In M. Gul, E. Celik, S. Mete, & F. Serin (Eds.), *Computational Intelligence and Soft Computing Applications in Healthcare Management Science* (pp. 42–62). IGI Global. doi:10.4018/978-1-7998-2581-4.ch003

Yue, H. (2018). Unstructured Healthcare Data Archiving and Retrieval Using Hadoop and Drill. *International Journal of Big Data and Analytics in Healthcare*, *3*(2), 28–44. doi:10.4018/IJBDAH.2018070103

Zanetti, C. A., George, A., Stiegmann, R. A., & Phelan, D. (2020). Digital Health. In R. Gotian, Y. Kang, & J. Safdieh (Eds.), *Handbook of Research on the Efficacy of Training Programs and Systems in Medical Education* (pp. 404–426). IGI Global. doi:10.4018/978-1-7998-1468-9.ch021

About the Contributors

Leo Eyombo, Ed.D., OD., MBA., Msc., MS., MA., obtained a doctoral degree in Health & Behavior Studies from Columbia University. Prior to this doctorate, he acquired a Doctor of Optometry, a Master of Science in Health Education, a Master of Art in Health Policy, a Master of Science in Public Health Education and a Master of Business Administration. In 2010, he completed post-doctoral fellowship in health Equity at the Columbia University. His multifaceted work experience consists of health care advocacy for the medically underserved, poor, uninsured and underinsured. He have developed primary health care programs both domestically and internationally, lobbying groups to develop and implement effective primary care programs for communities most in need. Other positions he held, has been a health care executive for a multiple specialty medical group, health care developer for primary care, health educator, and health care management faculty in the United States America (USA) and Asia (China-PRC). He have over fifteen year experience as a healthcare faculty and university administrator in the USA and PRC. These experiences includes curriculum development, health education, community health outreach, health policy, financial reporting, curriculum evaluation, education administration, teacher evaluation, Instructional learning strategies and health advocacy. As Chief Executive Officer for HomeworkXpress (HWX Group), for education technology and instructional learning. At Jinhua Professional Polytechnic University (JPPU) (CHINA), he served as Associate Professor in Business Management for the Chinese Exchange Program from 2012-2014. He is presently a faculty at Howard University in Washington, DC in the Department of Health Human Performance and Leisure.

Renee Murray-Bachmann is currently a nurse educator at Northwell Health System. She currently works to educate patients on diabetes.

Index

M

N

P

R

S

T

U

www.ingramcontent.com/pod-product-compliance
Lightning Source LLC
LaVergne TN
LVHW081519300926
849161LV00006B/1220
* 9 7 8 1 7 9 9 8 4 4 5 0 1 *